Preacher with a Plow

Preacher with

Plow

by Samuel B. Coles

Houghton Mifflin Company Boston
The Riverside Press Cambridge
1957

To my wife
BERTHA T. COLES
for her loyalty and dedication
to me and my work
during thirty years in Angola
and to my children
who sometimes thought me too exacting
with the Africans

Preface

In this book, I, Sam Coles, Alabama-born Negro of former African slave parents, have set out to chronicle my experiences of thirty years as an agricultural missionary for the Congregational Church in Angola, Portuguese West Africa. I have also attempted to tell something of the African native, his nature, his handicaps and his dreams as I saw them when I was working side by side with him in the lush, but largely wasted, river-bottom fields on the west coast of that vast continent.

Today I am at a crossroads and so is Africa. Having been retired from the missionary service I will soon return to Africa to lay the foundations for a Pestalozzi Children's Shelter (Agricultural and Industrial School for Orphans and Destitute Children) of Angola. It is difficult to imagine myself, an ox driver and blacksmith, pinning a diaper on a little five-pound baby, but I have had one rule in life — to do whatever the Master called me to do; and I shall undertake this new phase of service with the same fervent hope of helping the African people that I have had in my many years at the Galangue mission.

My plan is to take care of homeless children from all parts of Angola, but not to coddle or weaken them. We will keep them with us until they are eighteen, and by that time we will have trained them to make their own way with their hands and their heads. We will expect them to become leaders among the people of Angola and pillars in the religious life of the communities where they settle. Through our baby clinics, child welfare work and nursing schools, we hope to reach and save the lives of thousands of Angola babies and children each year. In the different departments of the school, shops and crafts of the farm and its connected church, we will train and develop young men and women for Christian leadership so urgently needed on the vast seething African continent.

Meanwhile I will be watching with intense interest and a little anxiety the development of Africa and the Africans. The African is becoming increasingly impatient and vocal. His grievances are manifold but his patience is extraordinary and his good humor expansive. The present danger, it seems to me, is not that the Africans will resort to violence but that they will so completely lose confidence in all outsiders that no constructive program of mutual endeavor will have any chance to succeed.

The outsider must meet the African where he is. In this book I have tried to show just where we can find him. We will need to take the African's hand and lead him gently through the unknown. That was what I tried to do.

One of the curses of the African is his laziness. As I

look back over my work and that of my fellow missionaries I would say that we have been too gentle with the natives. More than once I have told the Africans, "You don't work enough to perspire under your arms." They didn't like that but it made them get to work. Missionaries must preach in such a way as to provoke such thinking. Jesus Christ did. "Don't be afraid to cuss the Africans out," I say to the missionaries. The Africans need to be told bluntly what their shortcomings are and how they can be overcome. That has been the key to success of Negro institutions in the United States such as Hampton and Tuskegee and it's the kind of attitude that is going to move Africa and the Africans.

Anyone who wants to effectively help the African today must not merely point out to him how to become "civilized," but must show him the right way of living and doing things.

Often at our mission we tried to impress on the African: "That which doesn't hurt hasn't any value."

The missionary and Point IV workers alike, if they are to have any place at all in the future of Africa, will have to have their eyes open to the development of the people, instead of just a church or a system. Once they are on the right road, the people can develop their own church and their own government. At the same time the native must be made to see that wealth, blessings and civilization are not going to rain down on him from heaven. The "word" has got to rain into his heart and change his approach.

There have been some dark spots in our work in Africa but we, at Galangue, rejoice today to see our students working for the Portuguese government in responsible jobs and helping their own people as pastors and teachers as well as industrially. I rejoice especially that our students are doing effective work today in the field of agriculture. I am convinced that the first essential of a stable native country is agriculture. A native who is settled on the land is at his best. Away from it he is in trouble.

I want here to register my thanks to those who made it possible to initiate and maintain the work at Galangue station — especially to the American Board of Commissioners for Foreign Missions, the Superintendents of the Negro Congregational Churches, the late Dr. Alfred Lawless, the late H. S. Barnwell and the present tireless worker, the Reverend Joseph Taylor Stanley, because they have been the power behind the wheel.

The Galangue station today boasts of scores of young men holding Portuguese citizenship because they have successfully completed the required academic work enabling them to assimilate Portuguese customs. Today we have over one hundred and forty bush schools being taught by our graduates and former students.

Agricultural extension work has become a major part of our activity at Galangue. Practical carpentry and blacksmithing are being taught, giving us a Point IV aspect that is not common among Christian missions, but is I believe portentous.

I wish to thank Miss Mary Hornaday for her help in the technical task of writing this — my one-man Point IV story.

I also want to say thanks to those tireless workers, Dr.

and Mrs. H. C. MacDowell of Alabama, Dr. Aaron Mac-
Millan of Arkansas, Miss Lauretta A. Dibble of Wisconsin,
and the Reverend and Mrs. Maxwell Welch of Maine, all
of whom have left their homes to work among the African
natives.

And for the fact that an idea was born and has taken
hold now to the point where it can be of general help to
the world in solving one of its major problems I say finally,
in Umbundu, "Su-Ku-u-ne-ne. E-ye fu." ("Isn't God
big. He is eternal.")

S. B. C.

PUBLISHER'S NOTE

Mr. Coles died on March 9, 1957.

Contents

Illustrations follow page 82

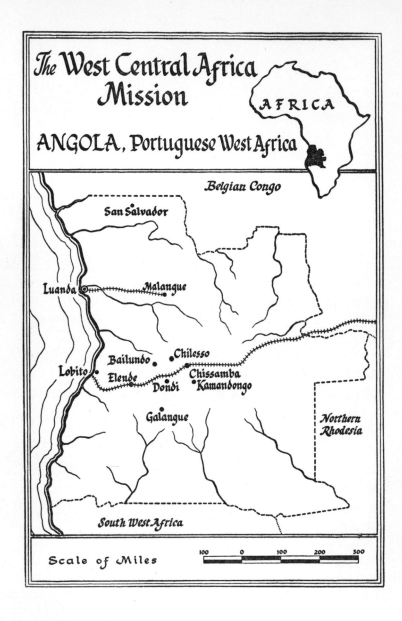

The West Central Africa
Mission

ANGOLA, Portuguese West Africa

AFRICA

Belgian Congo

San Salvador

Luanda   Malange

Bailundo   Chilesso

Lobito   Elende   Chissamba
Dondi   Kamandongo

Galangue

Northern
Rhodesia

South West Africa

Scale of Miles

100   0   100   200   300

I

From Blacksmith to Missionary

IT WAS "quiet hour" at Talladega College in Alabama one wintry Sunday afternoon back in 1912. A big husky Negro, twenty-four years old and finally starting to high school sat with his eyes glued to a remarkable little book — *Uganda's Man of Work, a story of Alexander M. Mac-Kay*, by Sophia Faha.

That was I — Sam Coles.

The people I was reading about were my ancestors — African tribesmen. Both my father and my mother had been born American slaves before the Civil War. Because they never went to school they were never able to read the kind of book that I was now reading but they had a simple, fervent love of God in their hearts and they had put it in mine. For this I shall always be grateful.

The book that made me decide to do something about Africans was given to me by my teacher, Ida F. Hubbard, a kind white lady, who came to Talladega from the State of Maine. I always like to call her my "missionary mother" because instead of making a doctor or a lawyer out of me as she did so many of her "boys," she saw something deeper and better in store for me. She said I was to be a missionary in Africa.

Before she handed me *Uganda's Man of Work* that day, the idea of Africa had never appealed to me. Africa, I had heard, was hot and full of wild animals and cannibals. Once when I was a child a man from one of the colonization societies had come and tried to get my father to go to Liberia. He told us there was "bread growing on trees" there; painted a glowing picture of this country where he said we, as Americans, would be members of the ruling class. At the time I put it all down as just big talk, and certainly nothing seemed more unlikely than for me to go to Africa.

Then I read about that brave Scotsman — Alexander MacKay. Things about the Dark Continent began to look different. MacKay was a wonderful man who answered a plea for help from Africans many many years ago. Back in 1875 when the American newspaper reporter Henry Stanley had just found David Livingstone in Darkest Africa, he came across King Mutesa in Uganda. The King began asking some questions about the white man's God. Stanley felt inadequate to answer them.

In a letter which was miraculously delivered to London and printed in a newspaper there, Stanley pleaded: "Oh that some pious practical missionary would come here!"

MacKay was one who volunteered to go. He was indeed an answer to Stanley's prayer for "a practical Christian who can teach people how to become Christians, care for their diseases, build dwellings, teach farming and turn his hand to anything."

MacKay, as it turned out, not only preached the word of God in a land groaning under the curse of the slave hunter but he made many useful articles with his turning lathe and primitive forge that delighted the hearts of the savages. Often his workshop was filled with tribal chieftains and slaves who gazed in amazement at the products of his simple tools.

What interested me most in *Uganda's Man of Work* was the part that told about MacKay finally being the only one left after the other missionaries had died or been killed. One day MacKay took two half oval parts from his steam launch and mounting them on six poles stuck in the mud floor made a wonderful table. After that he became a favorite of the King. Best of all was what a tribesman named Little Apollo said to him: "Now I can see your God because He is with you every day, even in the making of this table. I shall follow him."

The MacKay story unfortunately had a sad ending. His lot was a hard one. The King finally turned against him and kept him prisoner until his death at the early age of forty-one.

By the time I came to that part in the book I had decided that there were other kinds of missionaries besides preachers, doctors and teachers. As I closed the book that afternoon at Talladega, I told myself that if a man could be brought to Christ through the work of my hands, well, that threw new light on an idea that kept running through my head.

After that I read many books on Africa and gradually I became convinced that if more than three hundred missionaries had given their lives in Africa, certainly I should be willing to sacrifice myself, if necessary, to these my own people.

I had only one reservation about being a missionary in Africa. I didn't want to meet a lion. So far I never have, though I must admit there have been some other big and ferocious obstacles in my path at times.

While I was still at Talladega I began to get ready to go to Africa. I started building air castles. I have always thought this is all right because when they fall, at least they don't hurt you or anybody else. I even made one or two plows and singletrees for horses in the blacksmith shop just to get my hand in. I also made some large knives and could see myself chopping my way through the jungle with them.

My trip to Africa was delayed somewhat by the First World War which took me to France but then I graduated from Talladega with an A.B. in sciences, got myself married and finally sailed with my wife and baby daughter Laura, stopping off first in Portugal to spend nine months learning Portuguese, the official language of Angola.

I arrived in Africa in August 1923 to spend the next thirty years of my life there as an accredited missionary for the American Board of Congregational Christian Churches.

Our first stop was at Luanda, one of the finest cities on the West Coast. Here on an artificial isthmus lies a lovely seaside city. Leading back from it we saw the old caravan trail traversed by David Livingstone and many a white man's slave.

I shall never forget the first African student I met there

in Luanda at the Methodist mission where we spent a day and a night. He was just a little naked boy full of "itch" but he was a genius with figures, which is unusual for Africans. The teacher in charge took us into the classroom and asked my wife to call out numbers which the youngster squared, added and multiplied without a moment's hesitation. I was really enthused, and pulled out quite a roll of Portuguese money to give him. In American money, though, it was only worth about $2.50. Today that same boy is an outstanding minister in the Methodist Church in Angola and a missionary in São Thomé, one of the Portuguese islands.

My next early venture in humanitarianism in Angola was not so successful. I saw a young boy whose toes were raw and swollen. I was horrified and wondered what so small a boy could do to earn a heavy beating on the feet with a bamboo rod, which was the only explanation I could imagine. So I emptied my pockets to him and went away feeling I had paid a ransom for some man's cruelty. Imagine my embarrassment later when I began to see other boys with the same affliction and discovered that African "jiggers" had eaten their way under the skin!

Another of my early encounters was with a man whose stomach had been badly eaten by Congo maggots. The sores made a belt around his waist. This time I had already seen enough to be able to say: "My job is to better conditions so that this kind of thing cannot happen." Ever since the day I saw that man I have had deep in my heart the idea of making clay flooring tiles that can be laid in cement to form floors impervious to white ants and Congo maggots. They can be made by hand and any man will work enough to buy tiles if you once show him how they will relieve his physical suffering.

When I saw that man with the maggots eating around his waist, I remembered what General Samuel C. Armstrong, the founder of Hampton Institute, had said: "Do not give a man a dime which he can earn for himself but on the other hand train him and allow him a chance to earn it."

We moved from Luanda down to Lobito, one of the best ports on the entire west coast of Africa and terminus of the Benguela Railroad which was to take us inland. Lobito Bay is shaped like a horseshoe. During slave trade days, the white men's boats came in there and waited for cargoes, well sheltered from high tides and winds. The railroad was built by the British to bring copper, wheat and beeswax from Rhodesia and the Congo to ships waiting to carry it to Europe.

After clearing our baggage through the customs, we found a hotel which was very good — but it had "visitors." We were equal to that. We had a bottle of creolin with us. We took the mattress off and poured it into all the crevices and after that were able to sleep soundly.

When we left Lobito, I missed my train, but it was on purpose. We were headed for Nova Lisboa. I happened to see an African native bending over a telegraph key who was able to send by Morse code and this seemed so remarkable to me, I thought I should stop and watch him. I told my wife I would overtake the train at Benguela, the next stop, twenty miles away.

Just as I was to start out I was told that a lion — the last thing I wanted to meet in Africa — had come from the highlands into a village and killed a German woman. I had no arms with me but a walking cane, but there was nothing to do but go ahead. My path led through a sugar cane plantation and I can tell you I walked a good distance from the edge of that patch, figuring that if the lion came out I could give him a good wallop over the head and run. He didn't come, thank goodness. I think I set a record for speed that day, covering the twenty miles in three and a half hours.

It was very hot in the lowlands, although not as hot as we had expected. Supposing that all of Africa would be that sultry, we packed all our heavy clothes away in our baggage. The train started abruptly up a long hill so steep that it had to have an engine pushing instead of pulling it and cogs to keep it from slipping backwards. We climbed for two or three hours. As we climbed the rugged mountainside we saw many wonderful rock formations, and one or two baboons and a few monkeys among the sparse trees. The scenery was barren but beautiful. When we reached the summit the temperature had dropped to almost freezing and there we were without any warm wraps, except a bathrobe, even for three-year-old Laura.

As a rule the Portuguese stop at midnight and have something to eat. We ate at Catengue that trip. I was curious to see where the delicious sausage, rice, cabbage and coffee were being cooked so I wandered out of the railroad dining room into the detached kitchen nearby. My eyes fell on a native standing between the kitchen and dining room handing over the food. He wore about a yard of cloth and had evidently never taken a bath or combed his hair; but he didn't spoil my appetite. I was plenty hungry at that point.

Next morning about nine o'clock we arrived at Nova Lisboa. We had climbed a little over six thousand feet above sea level. There we were met by Dr. Henry C. McDowell, an American Congregational minister who founded the mission where we were to serve.

The idea of establishing a station in Africa where American Negro youth could work as missionaries among our own people was originally conceived by three men who received their own education in our mission schools in the southern part of the United States. They were the late H. H. Proctor, of the First Congregational Church of Atlanta, Georgia, the Reverend W. L. Cash, of the First Congregational Church of Thomasville, Georgia, and William H. Holloway, a Congregational minister now in Columbus, Ohio. These three men sent $100 to the American Board in 1915 as a nest egg for an African mission.

The American Board agreed to establish the mission but only on condition that Negroes should take on the entire responsibility. If they made good, it was explained, then the world would know it and if they flunked it would be their own fault. The American Negro Congregational Churches were told that they would have to support the work financially and enlist the personnel though it would be under the general supervision of the American Board. The Negro churches accepted this challenge.

Then came the job of finding the first family to go out. Signs pointed to Dr. H. C. McDowell who had just graduated from the theological department of Talladega College. When the committee broke the news that they wanted McDowell to go to Angola, he was startled, but as a Christ-like man he said simply. "Here am I. I am ready to go." He talked the matter over with his fiancée, Miss Bessie Farnville, who was teaching at the time in Athens, Georgia. She agreed to marry him and go with him. In August 1919, they set forth, along with a nine-month-old baby, Curtis F. McDowell, now a Chicago lawyer.

First they went to Chilesso where they stayed for three years, helping at the station there and learning the native language. Then they worked a year at Dondi, central training school for American and Canadian Board work in Angola.

Exploratory work for the Galangue mission site was done in 1920 by the late Reverend William G. Bell. When the Reverend Mr. Bell and his group visited Galangue they were received in great style. Presents were exchanged as is the custom of the country. At the time the ruler was Chief Chiquetekole, a powerful man who might at any time order a man's head cut off, and off it would go. The Portuguese were just beginning to get things under control in Angola then.

During their short stay in Galangue the Reverend Mr. Bell and his party did some preaching and reading of the Bible. The old chief's reaction was immediate: he told Mr. Bell that if the churches could not provide the Galangue people with a teacher at an early date he would abdicate his throne! That settled the question of where Dr. McDowell was to go.

So in 1922 Dr. McDowell staked off a concession near the village of Sende on the road leading from the Fort of Galangue due north to Nova Lisboa. It is about eighteen miles from the Ombala or royal village of Galangue. Later on, after some trouble with a rival mission, Dr. McDowell moved to our present site, near the village of Bunjei from which the mission derives its Portuguese name — Missião Evangélica de Bunjei. The present mission was opened January 15, 1923.

To meet us in Nova Lisboa, Dr. McDowell brought along a crew of African carriers from Galangue. When they saw me they stared with amazement because of my size. I am six feet tall and at that time was plenty fat. Their eyes bulging, they asked him what I had been eating. None of them had ever attained such avoirdupois on their simple grain and bean diet.

At this stop our baggage had to be repacked so it could be taken by the men on their shoulders. I didn't give the men credit for being able to tie up the baggage so I pitched in and started tying and sorting it. When I said I'd finished, they quietly proceeded to untie it all, then tied it up again. They did it one hundred per cent better than I had and I learned another lesson in the humility that I was to need in order to work among those people.

I got my first contact with a real cannibal's descendant when we started out for Galangue with Dr. McDowell in a brand-new Model T Ford. Our driver was a young man from the Essele country where the people through the ages have been cannibals. This man proved to be a careful driver and a good mechanic and we didn't need to worry.

Cannibalism has now been practically wiped out from the African continent, praise God.

Night comes quickly in Africa and it was after dark when we arrived in Galangue and were literally pulled out of the car by rejoicing natives. I was thrown onto the shoulders of the men and my wife and our little daughter Laura were placed in a hammock and carried all over the place by excited men and women. At long last, they cried, one of their own had returned to help them. The demonstration lasted about fifteen minutes and then, after they had taken us into the house, a mob pushed its way in and just sat and looked at us as though to say: "Well, you are one of us." Then they danced and sang some more outside the house.

Next morning after breakfast when we started to look around we found Dr. McDowell out calling the roll of his work gang. I had never seen such a sight in all my life. I could scarcely believe these men, women and children were to do the work. Many of them looked as if they should have been in a hospital bed, or at least having a good meal in some warm place. Their clothing was so sparse that my mind immediately placed them in a bedroom instead of a work line. What a picture they made!

Soon the sun came up and warmed the air, and the people were able to quicken their steps some.

Until our main building was ready that September, we lived in the dispensary. The floors were of dirt but well pounded down. Reed mats had been furnished to keep the dust down but soon we found that jiggers were making their homes in them. Our toes began to itch. Not knowing what the trouble was, we did nothing for several days, by which time our toes had become puffed like sausages. A young man was dispatched from the mission to relieve us of our misery. Careful though he was, the operation was about as painful as taking out a nail. One or two jiggers even got into the toes of our small daughter, Laura, and it was a real fight to get them out.

An African town or village is like nothing you have ever seen. The native huts are made of grass, shaped like tents, or of sticks and clay with a grass roof. Some of the grass huts are built on stilts to keep the spirits from walking in too easily. None of the houses have any windows as they would also make it easy for the spirits to find entrance. The people sleep on reed mats, which are made by the men of the tribe. In the center of the hut is a fire on which the woman of the house prepares the mush that is the mainstay of all the meals.

Most of both the men's and women's time is taken up in getting or preparing food. The men do the hunting but the women work the fields and do the threshing and preparing of the grain. They carry their babies on their backs while they work.

In late afternoon the women knock off from work in the fields and go home to prepare the evening meal, consisting of mush with a relish made of beans or other vegetables. The food is served in baskets. Each person breaks off a piece of hard mush and dips it into the relish. Sometimes the trays are washed in the stream and sometimes they're just licked by the dogs.

Then at dusk when the bats are beginning to swirl

around and you can hear the cry of hyenas far off in the distance, everyone goes to the "palaver house" where they listen to folk tales and tribal legends, guess riddles, and talk over the day's work until it is time to go to bed.

It was the dry season when we first approached Galangue but the country was beautiful even then. It is even more so after the rains have set in and the grass begins to green up. The rains begin the last of September and end in April or May. At first the new leaves are a light lavender color and remain that way until the heavy thunderstorms set in. Then suddenly they turn a bright, bright green. Flowers fill the air with perfume and, after a thunderstorm, the air is so fresh you have to breathe deeply, and find yourself wishing these storms would continue always.

After the first clamor surrounding our arrival had died down we had about two weeks of quiet and rest, but the show was not over. One bright afternoon about three o'clock I saw another mob approaching our abode. Dr. McDowell came and explained that the chief and his people had come to greet us formally and welcome us to their country. He asked me to give a little talk to them. Since I didn't know their language and they didn't know Portuguese, I spoke to them in English which Dr. McDowell translated into Umbundu.

I decided to take as my subject "The Word of God: Its Value and the Value of an Education." Maybe I was trying to show off a little with that subject. I had been sent out there as an "agricultural and industrial worker" but someway I felt I had to do a little preaching. I forgot to tell them I was also there to help them raise more food and get the simple necessities of village life, but I was soon pulled right down out of the clouds, kerplunk!

When I finished my sermon, the tribal chief of the area got up and asked a simple question: "Mr. Coles," he said, "do you have any corn in America which will mature within less than six months? That's what we need now because we're starving!"

Another tribal leader then got up, looked at me and said simply: "Mr. Coles, do you know that when there is hunger in a village the word of God is stalled?"

A third raised his voice: "Mr. Coles, hunger makes men do shameful things."

In a flash I saw the path my work there in Africa was to take. Certainly I meant no disrespect to the Almighty as I declared then and there with deep fervor: "Upon hoes, spades, shovels and seeds, I shall build my church and the gates of hell shall not prevail against it."

Since that day I have become more and more convinced that there is something lacking in a Christianity that widens horizons and creates new visions for men but fails to make its influence effective in assisting them to achieve these ideals.

The next few days I began to look around at the tribal lands. Here was a paradox. People were starving and without clothes. On the other hand, there was heavy, rich, dark earth in the river bottoms. It was some of the best farmland I had ever seen. Yet it had never been stirred with a hoe. Something was obviously wrong.

I asked the people why they were not cultivating this lush soil. First they said their backs would hurt if they tried to hoe the bottom lands. Certainly the sod was tough. This I conceded. Then they admitted they were afraid. Afraid of what? I asked. Of evil spirits, they said — the *Ondele* — the devil.

Evil spirits of what? Of their dead babies, they explained. In the river bottoms? Yes, they said. When their babies die they are buried in the river valleys so they will be near the water. Not having had time to walk, the babies had to be buried near the water, they believed, so their spirits when they wanted water would be near it. They must be able to lean over and drink easily.

If the tribe went down to work in those valleys, they would disturb the spirits which would then descend upon their mothers and cause them to die. Such was the tribal superstition.

Suddenly something came alive in my memory: hadn't my own father and mother told us when we were children back in Alabama that it was "bad luck" to go to bed without having water in your house, because your spirit might wake up in the night and want water? If it had to go down into the well or to the spring for it, your body would be left without a spirit for a while. During the time your spirit was out of the house, you were supposed to have all kinds of bad dreams.

Later on, when I was grown, I figured out that this superstition probably had gotten started because it was always a good idea to have a little water in the house in case it should catch fire, as our Negro shanties often did. Now it occurred to me that the belief had come from Africa. Who knows?

This superstition of my childhood gave me a certain respect for the seeming lack of rationality of the Ovimbundu tribe. At least I knew that with this belief implanted in their minds, it would be no use trying to use wordy persuasion on them.

I called the tribal leaders together and told them that hereafter a special place would be reserved as a burial ground. Above and below it we would cultivate. "God," I said, "will protect my wife, so I will plant first."

I got a few men to help me and we put under cultivation about five acres of land along the river. The tribesmen all watched our operation with fear and trembling. Fortunately after that first planting nothing happened to any of our wives.

In the early days of the mission our men didn't understand how to work with the tribesmen, and I remember when one of them, exasperated by the natives' passive resistance, had become so annoyed on one occasion that he got up and spoke his mind to an entire village gathering, scolding them in no uncertain terms. Later that day a trusted native hired man working at the mission came to warn him that some of the things he said that day could only make the situation worse. That was when our mission men first realized their own lack of tact. They knew they had a real problem to win the villagers over, and wouldn't get anywhere by issuing angry commands.

Gradually I began to work my way into their confidence. First I gave away hoes far superior to any ever used in that area. These made it easier to break the bottom grasslands. After that I announced I would offer prizes to those men who put under cultivation the largest pieces of land within a certain time. We measured the fields off by pacing them across and lengthwise.

In May, when the school closed for the summer, we gave out the farm prizes. The first prize winner received his tax money which came to $3.50, and the second a plow. When the others saw what I had done, they came clapping their hands and saying: "We have been thinking all along that you were a fool, but now we know it!"

"How is that?" I inquired. "Why," they said, "you have paid these men to work for themselves." I knew then that the taboos were broken. These people had begun to realize the value of those river bottoms. I would never have to offer prizes to get work out of them any more. Since then, I have given out such things as wheat and garden seeds but once the natives were able to see that just by planting in the valleys they could get two good crops a year, I never had to offer a prize again.

In the old days when they waited for the rains to wet the soil of the ridges, the local folk could not as a rule begin planting until October. Once they began to plant the valleys, they were able to sow their seeds as soon as the danger of frost was passed — about the last of July. By planting two crops they now have beans and squash the latter part of October and corn and beans the latter part of December. Also, more men have strength to work the fields and for the first time they have something to sell which gives them cloth for their wives and money for their taxes to the Portuguese.

Immediately after our arrival, my wife and I were faced

with the necessity of learning Umbundu, the language of the people among whom we were to work. Two native teachers were assigned to us. It wasn't easy. There were occasions when I had repeated a word so many times that my tongue would get so dry I thought I heard it rattling in my mouth.

The first thing we learned to say was, of course, "Good morning." In Angola if you meet a man coming along the road, you greet him "Tu-li-pasula" which is to say, "Let us greet one another this morning." If he feels like it, then he will say "Tu limbuka." Then both of you will throw out your chests and say "Kalunga-kalunga," several times.

The next thing we learned to say was "Food is ready" — "Oku-lia-quapia." That, believe me, was quite a useful phrase to know.

After we had been at Galangue only a few months, the McDowells left for America on furlough. They were gone ten months, which put us on our own in dealing with the natives. Many was the time a native would win a point by claiming not to understand our words. That way he could force a compromise. Those were a tough ten months but the experience proved to be worth all we paid. The following year we took our final examinations in the Umbundu language under the auspices of our missionary board and passed. As we became more fluent in their language, we came closer to the people.

When Dr. McDowell had opened the mission he had only one native family to help him. The first buildings were just three or four mud huts and a mud church where services were held every night. A little later a small band of local workers was recruited and a small class of night school students came together to be taught. They were mostly grown men who daytimes worked on the mission buildings and farm. As the work progressed and the night church services became more popular, there were at times more visitors than there was work.

The mission gradually grew larger and larger. In 1926, the church was organized by Dr. McDowell with an ordained African pastor whom he trained, and between two and three hundred members.

After our buildings were finished the masons and carpenters were at a loss to know what to do. Some of them thought they should go up to the city to find work. In the cities a good mason at that time was making from 75 cents to a dollar and a half a day. Here at the station we paid them only 50 cents a day, but they could live more cheaply in the village than they could in the city. In the city, a half bushel of grain cost 75 cents. In the village it could be bought for 40 cents and most of the men's wives raised their own meal so they got it for nothing.

One evening I called the men into the chapel. We got the blackboard down and figured out just how much a city man could save in a year when he worked every day and bought the things he needed. Then we took the same man and his family and put them to work on a farm. They cultivated corn, beans and wheat. They killed two or three hogs and sold the lard, making as much as $35 on a large hog.

I knew my talk had been successful when one day not long afterward our head carpenter came to me and said he'd decided he could do better on his farm than working at the mission. We suffered from the loss but at least he had been cured of the city's lure, one of the curses of rural Africa today.

That was a milestone in our effort to teach the people around Galangue, who love the bush and are rural at heart, that they are better off on their own fields than crowding into the cities where they fall prey to communism and other influences that are bad for them and for Africa's future.

2

A Ph.D. in Ox Driving

WHEN I WENT to Africa a record of my experience, if I had had to prepare one, would have read something like this:

"One and a half years laying steel rails; five years in logging camps, handling oxen and making bows and yokes; four years of practical dairying; three years in blacksmithing, horseshoeing and wheelwrighting; with various side experience in hewing timber, wood turning, canning fruits and vegetables, farm carpentry and brick masonry."

I have always said that the most valuable degree I took with me to Africa was a "Ph.D. in Ox Driving." I got that before I learned to read and write. While my formal education was an asset, working with those oxen when I was little more than a boy not only made me physically strong but taught me some valuable lessons I could never have learned from books.

My ability as an ox driver was my first passport to success among the African natives. It was something they understood, admired, and badly need at their present stage.

Africa, at present, is like a big dog. He is docile but if you step on his tail, he is likely to bite. Therefore white men and outsiders must be careful not to tread on his tail. That does not mean that more advanced people have to lower their standards of ethics or morality or give up their material comforts, even, when they go there. I only insist that they must be genuinely interested in teaching the African how to develop himself so he can better meet his own everyday needs. From my experience, I am convinced that this can easily be done.

I knew early in life that I wanted to be a preacher and it was this desire that finally took me to Africa. I was the second child of a family of three boys, born in Tilden, Alabama. My mother died when I was five, and my ten-year-old brother became the housekeeper.

My father usually took us to church on Sundays. I would listen to the preacher and I soon got to the point where I could repeat what he said. When we returned home I would preach to my brother who loved my sermons. Sometimes when he wanted me to preach, I didn't feel like it. Then we would enter into a deal. I would preach if my brother gave me a piece of bread or helped me with the wood for the stove or did me some other favor. Once I found that worked, I never happened to be in good preaching mood until he promised to do something for me. Then I would pay him with a ten-minute sermon.

I had to care for the cows and at times I practiced preaching to them. They never did pay off. They would run off with me or break the rope and make for the fields, which always meant a licking for me.

It seems odd that one of the nicknames given me in Africa should be "Yayulako" — the "hurry-up one." I suppose that is because I am an American and my tempo is just naturally faster than the African's. But when I was a boy I was the laziest cuss in three counties.

I was so lazy that my father would not take me with him to the fields when he went to chop cotton. He'd leave me home to see that the chickens did not ruin the garden. Looking for a way of doing that job more easily, I got the idea of cutting off the hens' claws so they couldn't scratch. I trimmed their bills, too, so they couldn't peck. When I was sure they couldn't hurt the garden any longer, I'd go off down the river to lie in the sun or fish.

Maybe out of some of that laziness, though, my patience was born. There is endless hard work to be done in Africa, yet one needs patience all day and every day.

My brother and I went to school in a one-room log building which was standard for Negroes in the South in those days. It had to accommodate all the children in the area.

Our attendance was poor. Usually we were there only a few days during the four or five months of the school year. We didn't have any mother to encourage us and Father was busy in the cotton fields.

One reason we didn't like to go to school was that our clothes weren't as clean or as good as those of the rest of the children. A sister of my father's who lived four miles from us did the washing. It was my job to carry the dirty clothes to her but it often turned out that for one reason or another I got there too late and then we had to go without clean clothes for the following week. My brother always remembered the fact that this was my fault and took it out on me by having me get more wood and water for the week than usual. When I rebelled, there was a fight. He always got the best of it because he was bigger. On top of that he would tell my father and that meant another licking.

I always attributed my hard lot in childhood to the fact that I was born in the middle of the family. When my mother died my younger brother was only a year old and he was taken to my grandmother on my father's side to be reared until he was eight or nine. He was safely cared for there and was never with us to help me with my heavy burdens. How I wished for him! Maybe he could have shared some of my troubles. I decided that if I could be born again I would choose to be either the first or the last. I didn't like being in the middle.

When I was old enough to chop cotton I was given a hoe and my brother a plow. The mules pulled the plow so all my brother had to do was walk behind it and sing. But poor me! I really had to work. The best way out, I decided, was to do as little as possible. When my father had had about as much of my playing and crying as he would stand, he would pull down a gum bush and snatch a brush off it and sail into me. Then I would quicken my step for the rest of that day, at least.

A storm in June 1900 destroyed all the crops of our area and about half of the homes. Although our home was not blown away, our crop was ruined. We planted again but it was too late in the season to get a good crop. We were sharecroppers and that fall the man who had been "furnishing" my father with food and the mule came and took everything we had — even our cattle.

After that my father took my older brother and went to work on the railroad that ran from Selma to Linden, Alabama. I felt disgraced because my father left me with his sister and mother, and I decided to follow. I caught up just as the menfolk's train was leaving for Selma. When my father saw me he yelled to me to go back home. How I cried! Then the other men on the train begged my father to let me come on. When the word was given the train was already hitting it up about fifteen miles per hour. I threw my little bag on the platform, then I moved faster than I ever had in my whole life to catch the rear coach where a man pulled me on.

I realized then that my next big job was to prove to my father that his lazy good-for-nothing son was as much a man as his eldest.

We laid track and I was made water boy. I carried water for six months but every chance I got I would grab a shovel and work until someone called for "water boy." Then fortunately a boy smaller than I came looking for a job. He was made water boy and I was promoted to a shovel. The pay I got was the same as the men's then — 75 cents a day and my pork and beans. After I got my new job, unbeknown to my father, I tried my luck at some 10-cent craps and also did a little harmless swearing. Some of those men in our gang were hardly fit companions for a would-be-preacher, but I recall that there were also a few very fine ones.

After I learned to drive railroad spikes I could send one

down in what we called "two licks and a tap" along with the best of the men. The two men who operated the gang wanted to take me home with them to live in Montgomery, Alabama, so I could go to school, but my father would not agree to it so my education had to wait a while longer.

In the fall of 1903, when my father returned home to get married, I determined to leave and go to my maternal aunt in Pensacola. The problem was to raise the money to get there. I went to my father's sister who had been keeping our money and told her my father wanted $10 just to have in his pocket on his wedding night. She gave it to me, and already suffering deep agony over the lie I told, I left the house at three o'clock in the morning.

That was the first time I had ever been out at that hour alone. I felt as though all the spirits of the other world were on the road to catch me. Even after daybreak I could practically see and feel my father coming behind me and every ten or fifteen yards I was compelled to look back to see if he was in sight. I reached my aunt's home in Pensacola at three o'clock in the afternoon and stayed six months, working on the railroad and the docks.

The black sheep in my aunt's family was an uncle who was a professional gambler. He decided to teach me the trade, but we had to have some money so we signed up on a railroad gang. Three days later my uncle got into some trouble with one of the bosses and had to skin out of the camp in a hurry. That night when I came back from work I found him gone. He had left word for me to follow so I took off parallel to the railroad but stayed deep enough in the woods not to be seen by anyone who might have been pursuing us. Finally I caught up with him.

In that part of Florida, near the Alabama border, there were signs posted in those days which said: "Negro, read and run. If you cannot read, run anyway." So we kept on going.

At eight o'clock that night we came to a logging camp where there was a big dance on. We thought maybe we could get work there. A man came out but when he discovered we were Negroes, he said: "Boys, get away from here as fast as you can because if the other men see you, there will be trouble for you."

This was a new experience for me. The fear that crept over me nearly sent me into a convulsion, but I followed my uncle into the woods. That night we spent under a large pine tree and my uncle snored so loudly I was sure someone would find us. But they didn't. For breakfast we had ripe blackberries.

It was then my uncle decided to teach me to eat from the "kitchen of the public" as we called it. Most people called it hoboing. It meant going to the back door of a house and asking for something to eat. Being young, I usually had pretty good luck. Often my offer to carry a pail of water or get in some wood in payment wasn't accepted either.

We walked along the railroad for eight or ten days, eating berries and living off handouts. My shoes wore out and my uncle told me I would have to steal a pair, but the teaching of my father was still strong in me. I told my uncle I just could not do it. He insisted the time would come when I would be forced to, but I said the time had not yet come.

In that brief hoboing experience, I saw one thing that

was valuable to me later on in Africa. I saw how hunger and poverty can lead one to be tempted to do things he would otherwise have no inclination to do.

Finally both of us found work on a section gang near Tunnel Springs, Alabama. I worked regularly but my uncle chiefly waited for his gambling game on payday. One day when he happened to be working, a young white man in the gang grabbed his shovel so it would look as if he were working when an inspection man suddenly rode past on a passenger train. Next day we were tipped off by another white man that a posse was coming to get my uncle and give him a good beating for "telling off" that man, as he did after the train was past. When we told my uncle what was in store for him, he took my new undershirt and a few other things and left.

Thus, one of the worst influences of my early life walked out of it. I have never seen him since but I have many times thanked my lucky stars that I wasn't led downhill any further by him. The teaching of my dear father had really stuck.

Next I went to work in a logging camp that belonged to the Bay City Lumber Company of Mobile. There I learned to drive oxen.

My, those were fine teams — those six oxen and the driver. I can see them now as they "snaked" those big pine logs through the rough underbrush into the road where the oxcarts picked them up. Eventually the logs were taken to the Alabama River where they were rafted and floated down to Mobile.

At first I was not allowed to handle the oxen. My job

was to set the tongs in the logs for the driver. John Daniels with whom I worked was one of the greatest ox drivers I have ever seen. Of course, my ambition was to drive, too. So I watched for opportunities.

Gradually they came. Daniels let me take the oxen to water with their yokes on and drive them to the camp after work and bring them back out in the morning. Also, sometimes Mr. Daniels got a little too much of payday's "coffee" in him and would not show up for work for two days. Then the boss of the camp let me take the team out and skid logs, and I had another boy hitch the tongs for me. Boy, was I thrilled when John did not show up on Monday mornings! I could hardly wait to start driving.

When an ox did not pull as John thought he should, he always swore at him, so I learned to cuss as part of the trade. The two lead oxen were "Mike" and "Sam." The two in the "swing" were "Little Spot" and "Charlie." The two rear or chain oxen were "Frank" and "Big Spot." When I thought Frank or Sam was not pulling I would roll out a strong cuss word at him. I waited until I was out of hearing of the men, then let the poor oxen have it. With a roar I threatened to kill each and every one of them. I don't know whether my bellowing had much effect on the oxen but it sure developed my lung power.

John could see how badly I wanted a team of my own so he told the boss. Soon I was allowed to go to the lot and pick me a team from among the "dead-heads." These were oxen which had been knocked out for one reason or another. Some were too old to work. Some were blind. I picked the best of the lot, but alas, when I got my team of eight together, I had only one good eye in the lot. Anyway, I yoked them together, got my cart with wheels six feet high and went into the woods hopefully. I backed up to the first log my size, jacked it up and started off. It took me just about twenty-four hours to get to my destination. When I got onto the road, my wheels went down in two feet of mud and my oxen decided they just would not pull.

I cried big tears, cussed at the top of my voice and beat the poor things for all I was worth. Noon came. I unhitched them and led them to water, then to the camp where they rested and I ate. That evening I took them back to work but the results were the same. The next day a man with his team came and pulled me out. I was mortified but I was also determined. I knew those oxen had to be educated.

For the next three or four weeks, I backed that team to the smallest log I could find. By doing so, I got them used to walking in the road and pulling. Pretty soon that team, tag ends though they were, was of some real use. From then on I went places.

Later on I was chosen one of the best ten drivers on the job. Those first hard days had paid off. I often thought of that experience when I ran into trouble in Africa trying to drive those people that I had come to help too far and too fast.

It was about that time I learned to read and write. My home town girl friend, Della Martin, was able to read and write but she knew that I couldn't. One day when I was home from the logging camp on vacation she said: "If only you could read and write, how much more I could tell you!" I thought to myself she had been telling me enough but if more could be gotten by being able to read and write, I decided to acquire that art. So I went to Camden, Alabama, the county seat of Wilcox County, to Mr. Liddell's store and bought a second reader, one of the McGuffey series. I ought to have gotten a primer but the second reader was cheaper so I bought that. They let me enter the little summer school in Camden. I knew my letters but nothing about sentences or words. I committed that book to memory in three weeks' time, then I went back to the logging camp where I discovered I could address my letters, read them and so on. I was eighteen when I learned to read and write. Of course, the first entire sentence I learned to write was: "Darling, I love you."

Then I found I still didn't know enough. I was invited because of my good nature and character to join a Masonic order. When I got into the order I bought a book of the ritual but there were parts of it I could not understand, because I didn't read well enough. Also I had been hearing about bricklayers earning four dollars a day and I thought it would be wonderful if I could go to school and learn that trade or some other.

One day a Mr. J. R. Wingfield, who at the time was principal of Lomax and Hanner High School of Greenville, Alabama, came to preach at the camp where we were cutting timber. After the sermon he asked how many of us would like to come to night school. The following Monday five of us entered his school, but after two weeks I was the only one left. Sometimes it was as late as nine o'clock when I could get to "school" but that fine man, Professor Wingfield, always had time to hear my lessons.

One night after class I made the remark that I would like to go to Tuskegee to school but did not have enough money. "Why," said the professor, "you don't need money because you can go to night school and work in the daytime to earn your way through. Look at me," he said. "I went to night school for four years and learned a trade. From the trade I earned enough to go into day school."

That planted some new thoughts in my head. I said nothing, but I told myself: "If he did it, I can too."

About a year later our camp moved to Lower Peach Tree, Alabama, and there I came into contact with two young men who were students at Snow Hill Industrial and Normal School, at Snow Hill, Alabama. They came to help in our Sunday School. Snow Hill was just seven miles from where I was born and reared but all I had heard of it in my younger days was that the boys there were not given much to eat. I had decided early that it was no place for me, but now I began to look at things in a different light. These two boys were well dressed, "talked grammar" as we said, and generally made a good impression. I came to the conclusion that if they could survive the meager dining facilities at Snow Hill and look the way they did, I could do the same.

Finally in September 1908, at the age of twenty, I told the boys in the logging camp goodbye. I was going to school.

They told me: "Kid, you are too old. You can't learn anything."

I replied: "Well, I'll die trying."

When I left the camp I had $150. It occurred to me that I might put it to work and make more by lending it to a friend who was opening up a little store. A few months later when I thought I should be having a dividend, I found he had spent it all buying himself a home. Shortly after that he died and I never did get my money back.

When I learned that my money was gone, I asked the Master to show me what to do. This thought flashed through my mind: You have made lots of money in your lifetime, but you don't have it now. Go back to school and stick it out at any cost.

That first year at Snow Hill I worked in the kitchen with the two young men I had met in the logging camp. They taught me to bake bread and make rolls. Besides the work I did for the school dining room, on the side I would buy five cents worth of flour, five cents worth of lard and some sugar and make it into light rolls that I sold to the boys at night. I made about seventy-five cents on each batch. That meant I netted sixty cents, not counting my time.

I went almost immediately into the fifth grade at Snow Hill but more than once I felt like returning to the logging camp. Then would come that still small voice saying, "Stick to it," and I would take on fresh courage and try again. Where I used to drive oxen in my sleep, now I conjugated verbs and sometimes I got them all mixed up together.

They say when you dream about a thing you are getting to understand it. That must have been true with me because when school opened the following year I skipped a grade and entered the seventh, and soon got to where I understood the work.

For those who know those two fine Negro institutions, it will be enough to say that my professors at Snow Hill were graduates of Tuskegee and Hampton Institutes. Snow Hill was founded by Professor W. J. Edwards, a graduate of Tuskegee who had worked his way through school. His education had been won against heavy odds: at one point, when he was a young man, he injured his arm so severely that he gave up all his hopes and asked the Master to take his life, believing he would be permanently crippled. But he got better and worked a little farm where he raised some cotton, sold it, and used the money to go to Tuskegee Institute. Professor Edwards took a great interest in me. He always told me to "stick to it."

I was at Snow Hill for four years. The first year I worked in the kitchen and the next three in the blacksmith shop. I never did learn the bricklaying trade that had lured me to school but blacksmithing was something that was to serve me well later in Africa. It enabled me to bend iron — and that was the basis of much of my work as a practical missionary in Africa. I never could have made those plows, oxcarts, wheelbarrows and ditching plows, or taught the African natives how to make them if it had not been for the blacksmithing I learned at Snow Hill. I was being trained for a mission I knew nothing of at the time.

During the fall of 1911 the main dormitory for girls at Snow Hill burned. The Reverend R. A. Daily, who had charge of the buildings and grounds, was sent to various schools in the state to study different types of buildings best suited for the girls. One of the places he went was Talladega College. When he returned and read his report it was so dazzling and inspiring that I thought right away I should like to go there and learn to be a civil engineer.

Another reason I had for wanting to go at that time was to see white teachers teaching Negro students. I could hardly imagine that. I was determined to see with my own eyes the white man Christ-like enough to teach and eat with Negroes. 1016770

The interracial pattern of Talladega College is as old as the eighty-seven-year-old institution itself. A clause in the school's charter of February 1867 proclaims it "A school from which no one shall be debarred on account of race or color." At Talladega, the interracial ideal has been consistently practiced. The chartering group was interracial and from the beginning the trustee board has been and still is, interracial. Until recently both elementary and high school departments were maintained on the campus for Negro and white students. Today the school, though located in the Deep South, is still interracial through the ninth grade.

This may not seem so strange now that the United States Supreme Court has desegregated the races in the public schools of the South, but when I was a boy entering an interracial school was like being thrust suddenly onto another planet.

I arrived on the Talladega campus June 12, 1912. It was suppertime and I was taken to Foster Hall. I was hungry before I entered the building but when I walked in and saw all those white and black people eating together I could not eat for looking around and wondering what in the world was to come next.

When I entered Talladega College, I had had three years in blacksmithing at Snow Hill, so I was made a student-teacher of blacksmithing. Not only did I teach that subject for two years, but with two other students, C. M. Powell and C. E. Rambo, I did all the farm repair work for the college. This way I was able to earn my board and tuition, but I had to work hard to do it.

The summer of 1913, I worked in the mines in Birmingham, Alabama, and made enough money to pay my next year's tuition, get a suit of clothes, buy my books and still have a little spending money left over. That soon gave out and I had to look for some other job to supplement my shopwork for the next school year.

One night the Reverend C. Harvey Robinson, who had charge of the college dairy, announced that he needed someone to help with the milking. I asked him how much he would pay for the milking of eight cows. He said $8 a month, so the following morning I went to the dairy barn. Mind you, I had never before milked more than one cow at a time. It made me tired even to think of those eight, but there were two more young men working in the barn and they helped me at first. After two weeks I had the cows quite under control. Sometimes, especially during the football season, it looked as if I might be left behind in my studies, with all this extra work, but my teachers were kind and helped me keep up.

Soon I began to think of ways to save the college money.

When I took over the work of the dairy three men worked there and the food for the hogs was bought. I said I could do the work alone and would plant enough peas and rape and millet so they could stop buying feed from outside. I used these crops sparingly, fed the hogs scraps and really had fat animals when butchering time rolled around. The college did not have to spend a dime on them for the whole three months.

Also I introduced a system of mule feeding that I had learned in the lumber camps which cut down considerably on their intake and kept them well so they could work even better than they had before. When the men brought in something broken at noon I took it to the shop and fixed it while they ate so it would be ready when they went back to work in the afternoon. For this landslide of work I was paid the grand sum of $27 a month, without food. I drank all the milk I could hold and that cut down on my food bills some.

Still the money wasn't enough to make ends meet so I could stay in school, so I went out and picked plums and berries and made them into jams. These I sold to the boys who came back loaded with money when school opened in the fall and to some of the faculty, like Miss Hubbard, the wonderful woman who first interested me in becoming a missionary. On the side, too, I had a garden of an acre or more that I cultivated at night with the help of Old Pete. He was a good mule.

It was at Talladega that I began to read and study about a great American — General Samuel Chapman Armstrong, founder of Hampton Institute.

General Armstrong was the son of a missionary. Right

after the Civil War, when he was assigned as an agent under the Freedman's Bureau to ten counties in Virginia, he started the Hampton Normal and Agricultural Institute. Through his own tireless efforts and tremendous self-sacrifice, it grew into a great school for Negroes.

One of General Armstrong's famous sayings was this: "The North generally thinks that the great thing is to free the Negro from his former owners. The real thing is to save him from himself."

I used to pore over General Armstrong's writings by the hour. What my people needed, he said, was to gain self-respect through working with their hands. He knew we were different from the white man. He recognized us as a race that had had little necessity to work in their native land before being forced to come to America. After coming here, our forefathers were forced to labor 250 years under circumstances that had not made them particularly fond of hard work. Yet work he felt was really our salvation, though he wanted to see thought and skill put into it to lift it out of drudgery. As I worked long hours in those barns and fields at Talladega his words inspired me.

"Labor," he said, "next to the grace of God in the heart, is the greatest promoter of morality and the greatest power for civilization."

He knew my people liked to sing and dream but he said we needed to be good farmers and mechanics instead of poets and orators. "The temporal salvation of the colored race for some time to come," he said once, "is to be won out of the ground."

General Armstrong was a man who would go through

any hardship to accomplish an aim. When things looked black to me and I seemed to be drifting instead of making progress toward a goal I thought of a story of General Armstrong's. It went like this: "Once there was a woodchuck. Now woodchucks can't climb trees. Well, this woodchuck was chased by a dog and came to a tree. He knew that if he could get up that tree the dog could not catch him. Now woodchucks can't climb trees, but this one had to, so he did!"

Nobody could have understood what I, Sam Coles, was to be up against, when my days at Talladega finally led me to far-off Africa as a missionary. My Talladega teacher, Miss Hubbard, inspired me to enter that work, but General Armstrong's words furnished the guide I was to need in trying to get other black men, a few notches below even me on the economic ladder, to the point where they could help themselves and no more live on the verge of starvation and death.

He was a great man and a benefactor to all of us Negroes both here and in Africa.

3

Apostle of the Plow

THE HARD manual labor I had become accustomed to as a child, and the skills I'd acquired in order to work my way through college, stood me in good stead from the very beginning of my career in Africa.

When the American Missionary Association gave Dr. McDowell $9000 and the Plymouth Congregational Church furnished $900 for a girls' dormitory, we began to build our permanent plant at Galangue. About $6000 of the $9000 went to build Brownlee Hall which is used as a school and chapel. The rest covered three boys' dormitories and two shops. In addition, friends of Dr. McDowell and a number of young people contributed some $1900 toward a residence for him.

We divided up the work of the mission. Dr. McDowell took charge of the "general station work," which is more or less the catch-all department, including the evangelical work, all the building supervision and the handling of money, books, supplies and cloth. Mrs. McDowell took charge of the school, maternity work and the day nursery. My wife had charge of the girls' boarding department and the women's work.

My major job was in the field of agriculture, though I also had charge of the boys' boarding department, the supplying of building material such as the hauling of rocks for the building foundations and the cutting and hauling of lumber. For seven years I was also in charge of the mission's medical work.

There were times when we were forced to go as far as forty miles away to get timber to use as trusses for our largest buildings. Because we had oxcarts we were able to get timber ourselves for less than half what it would have cost if we had had it brought in by men on their shoulders. In marshaling those oxcarts, of course, I was right in my element.

We cut a lot of timber on the Cunene River near the village of Musungu, about twenty-five miles from the mission station. I had to go there to measure it up for the men to cut with long pit saws.

One of the early trips taught me a lesson I shall long remember. I had been in the habit of carrying food from home on these trips but one day I took along my dog and a young man. I divided my lunch with them so that it did not leave much for me. On the way back I was so hungry I could see biscuits floating around in the air in front of me. About four o'clock in the afternoon I was still six or seven miles from home.

Soon I came to a village where the people knew nothing about household science the way we were teaching it at the mission. I asked them for something to eat. They looked at each other and said they didn't have anything. I told them whatever they had for themselves would be good enough for me.

Then I heard one man mention the word *ochisangua* which is a sweet beer the people make by putting meal in hot water and letting it stand overnight. The container in which it was handed to me looked as though it had never been washed. The ochisangua was full of flies and gnats.

One man took a piece of straw from the thatched roof of the house and started picking things out of the beer. First he blew on the basin to bring the extraneous bits together so he could get them out faster. He picked and picked but could not get them all.

I decided that a few bugs' legs would do me no permanent damage, so I took the bowl of beer. As I started to drink I could see the legs flying both right and left and some coming up from the bottom for good measure.

I shut my eyes and closed my teeth to try to strain out the extra matter some. Then I took a drink.

As I did so, I heard the people around me saying in their native tongue: "Why, he will eat with us!" Their joy was such that I realized I could not have created as much satisfaction with a dozen sermons.

That night when I got home I told Bertha that never again would I take a lunch with me. From then on when I went to a native village I always ate with the people.

Gradually I began to work my way into peoples' confidence in other ways.

When our mission station was opened in 1923, some of

the men we came to help were from one to three years in arrears with their taxes. With tax day always staring them in the face with its penalties, life was a nightmare for most of the natives. I saw and understood their plight immediately but what could I do about it?

When I first started visiting around among the old men, I told them jokingly that if I had a sack large enough I would put all of them in it and drag them to the ocean and throw them in. "If I could get rid of you," I told them, "the young men would have a chance to develop and be somebody."

In Africa the whole life of the young men is governed by the old men. They do most of their thinking for them and tribal traditions and rules are so strict there is not much chance to get any advanced ideas across to the young men.

Since I soon saw it was impossible to separate the young men from the old, I told myself I would have to work out ways and means to influence them and thus woo them away from their fathers and uncles.

I knew that I had come among them not as one who could beat their sins out overnight even if I wanted to, but as one who would have to be deeply concerned with their whole way of life and well-being, if I wanted to make any lasting progress toward a better life for these Africans.

I set out to find out what was causing them the most trouble. Invariably, their No. 1 problem was tax money.

Hunger usually came second, and lack of clothing third.

I could see, too, that they had big hurdles of apathy and superstition. It was going to take plenty of presently unused elbow grease as well as planning to get rid of these, I knew.

Some of the men worked very hard while they were in the fields but it was late when they got there and they didn't stay very long.

I told them — "You go to the field now at ten or eleven o'clock in the morning and return home at three or four in the afternoon. Although you may work hard while you are there, you have not 'put enough sun' into the field. What you are going to produce during the short time you are there is only enough to pay your taxes." I told them, "You won't have enough left over for food and clothes. Remember," I said, "that the rats are going to get their share while the corn is in the field and the wild animals will come, too. After they have taken theirs there will not be enough to take care of your other guests when they come to visit you, to say nothing of the Ochimbanda — the witch doctor — who is always looking for his pay."

I marked off in the eastern sky where they should begin with the sun, showed them just where the sun should be before they began resting for the noon hour, told them how long to rest and when to get up and begin working and then pointed out where the sun should be standing when they stopped to go home.

I told them that the first hour they added to a day's work they had to give to the rats and wild animals. Then the next hour's work we figured was for their visitors, the next for the witch doctor, the next for taxes and then all that was left was their own for food, clothes, bicycles and so forth. That way we planned together that they should reach the fields by seven in the morning and not leave for home until four o'clock.

In Angola, it is generally accepted that it is the wife's duty to feed the family, while it is the man's job to get the tax money and furnish the clothing. So I had to encourage and cajole the women, too, so as to get them to give their husbands and children enough to eat.

When I went into a village I would go and open the corncrib door. If there was no corn there or I could see the bare floor showing through, I would tell the women that their husbands were not bringing them nice things from their trips any more because they were not being well fed at home.

To get those little extra pretties, I said, they must add a few more hours to the sun. When they did, they could give their menfolk heaping plates of corn meal mush, with lots of good gravy.

Then I said they should sit off and watch the ears of their husbands moving eagerly up and down as they ate the big platefuls, and I'd illustrate with my own ears. How they would laugh!

The job of the woman was toughest because when there was not enough food the tribespeople would look down upon her and say she was lazy, but if the family had no clothes, the man would merely say, "Epele ka levala" — "nakedness does not hurt" — and would go merrily on his way.

Despite all the good advice they heard from me, most of the people did not get into the fields at seven o'clock in the morning of their own accord. I had to put extension workers in the villages. One of their jobs was to see that by seven there was not a male to be found in the village. And not a man was allowed to show his face again before five o'clock in the evening. At first the men shook their heads and said: "Oku linga upange ndoto, chivala inene" — "To work like that, it hurts indeed." But soon they truly learned to say: "Ka chivala ka chikuete ondando" — "If it does not hurt, it has no value."

All the years I was in Angola, I stayed close by the people's side, encouraging them to cultivate those rich, wasted river bottoms and to chide them when they started to backslide in this great work of pulling themselves up by their own bootstraps. Their increased plantings created a scarcity of the best land, so soon it was necessary to drain the marshland. This gave us a chance to remove the breeding place for mosquitoes.

I found it was best first to deal with simple things, to begin with what the natives know and drive home all the points with humorous and picturesque language. It is one thing to start something on a small scale and keep it going oneself with a handful of helpers, but to expand the scheme to a large scale and have it become indigenous and self-propagating — that is something else again. We had two main objectives in our farm work: (1) to have cash crops at the right season, (2) to have surplus grain for seeds for the next crop.

When I went into a village on a weekend I would usually preach Sunday mornings and in the afternoon a hundred or more men and I went out to look the river-bottom fields over.

When we came across a field about an acre in size I

would say to the man to whom it belonged: "Man, you
are a good American!" They always got a big kick out of
that praise. When the field was small, I would tell the
owner that he was just another lazy African. The men
seemed to work largely to please me. That was a great
challenge to me to keep them on the right path.

Sometimes after preaching on Sunday in a village, I
talked to the people about increasing the variety of their
crops and about village sanitation. I sometimes repri-
manded the men for making the women do too much of
the hard work. In order to put this idea across, I would
say to the women that if I were an African woman I would
not marry an African for anything. They would ask why.
I would reply that any time I brought a child into the
world for a man and he sat down and let that child starve
to death, he was less than a man. I would not marry him.
I told them that any man who merely sits around at home
and blows into the fire, as I had seen some of them do, was
less than a man, and I would not marry him. As soon as
they saw the point, they would not let me scold them
long. Whenever I'd start they would say : "Ah, Sekulu,
ku ka chipopia vile lombololaño, chilingiwa" — "Do not
curse us more. Explain what you want and we will do it."

When I first talked to the men about working their
oxen, they were amazed. To the Ovimbundu, cattle are a
symbol of wealth — and that's all they are, until the day
they're butchered. They accumulated large herds back in
the days when they were great warriors and plunderers.
Even today, the more cattle you have, the richer you are,
and the animals were treated with the greatest consideration; the natives actually never milk their cows, so that

the calves will grow strong and fat. They complained that the yokes we provided were too heavy for the oxen's necks. I would say, "But the hoe is not too heavy for your wives and a bag of corn is not too heavy for your wives to carry forty or fifty miles to the market." They had no answer for that. Then I would tell them they should work their oxen so they could save the backs of their wives. They saw what I was saying was true and began to act accordingly. Now they have absorbed the idea that it is the ox's place to work. In other words, the cattle have been dethroned in Galangue and their place of distinction given to men and women.

I kept driving home my point, saying: "There are shirts everywhere, but not a shirt for you to wear. There are good warm overcoats everywhere but not one for you to wear. There is tax money everywhere but none for you to pay your taxes. There are bicycles everywhere, but none for you to ride. There are warm blankets everywhere, but there is not a single one for you to cover yourselves.

"But if you will let hoe down where you are, there you will find tax money, shirts, overcoats, blankets, shoes and bicycles."

I introduced shovels and told them the shovel was their "silent doctor."

As a rule, I would close each pep talk with the words of my first sermon: "Upon these hoes, spades, shovels, seeds and plows, I shall build my church and all the gates of hunger, fear from the lack of tax money, superstition, poverty and nakedness shall not prevail against it."

When I went to Africa in 1923, slavery was still practiced there though it had been officially abolished by the government sixty-two years before. In 1885, Portugal joined with Great Britain, Austria-Hungary, Belgium, Denmark, France, Germany, Italy, Netherlands, Russia, Spain, Sweden and Norway, Turkey and the United States in the Treaty of Berlin to write the "rules for the future occupation on the Coast of Africa." This treaty said that any power which took possession of a territory on the coast of Africa thereafter must notify the other treaty signatories and must maintain sufficient authority "to enforce respect" for their acquired rights and for freedom of commerce through the area.

Also included in the treaty was an agreement to put an end to the slave trade in the areas belonging to the signatories.

On one of my homeward trips from Liberia, the ship put in at Matadi up the Congo River and I saw there deepworn foot paths, down which many of my people had been marched to be sold into slavery. That day I could almost see and hear the lash on the back of some poor woman who could walk no farther. I could see the long line of men as they were marched chained together across the long, hot plains. Many of them had been men of high rank in their villages but they had been captured in battle by an army more powerful than their own and sold so they would not cause any more trouble in the land.

Even in 1923 some parents were selling their own children as slaves just because they were hungry and saw no other way of getting enough to eat for their little ones.

Soon after my arrival in Angola, I remember, a fifteen-year-old girl came frantically to the mission one day seeking freedom. She was pursued by an old man and a chief who came from a neighboring village to fetch her. Naturally, being a minister of the gospel, I berated them in stiff language and befriended the girl. With a great flourish I got out the law abolishing slavery and read it to them. I ordered them out of the mission and informed them that if they came back I would tell the local officials. That day the girl — Nachilulu — told me there were nineteen slaves in our village, Bunjei.

I decided that I must set them free and one day, with the whole mission crew at my side, I set out on this philanthropic project. There was quite a dramatic scene as I called out the name of the slaves and lined them up on one side of the road with their masters on the other and proceeded to read the Portuguese law in a pontifical voice. In the exhilaration of the moment, I fancied myself a black Abraham Lincoln.

Then I learned something from the people I hadn't known before. One of the Christians in the village stepped up and explained to me that if I forbade those slaveowners to keep slaves in their village they would only send them two hundred or so miles away and make them slaves away from their own people and familiar surroundings.

Slavery, I learned, came about this way. A hard-pressed man whose children were hungry would borrow money or cattle or corn from a friend and then transfer the custody of his child to that person. Then he would work hard to redeem his child.

If I insisted on doing away with slavery, it would only mean the children would be shipped away to a neighboring tribe. They would still be slaves and worse still would be living among strangers with a strange language.

I admitted my eyes had been opened to their point of view. I wiped off my mouth pensively and turned to the slaves. I put the burden of their plight not on their owners, but on them. Squarely. "You," I told them, "must work and get money to pay your ransom so you can be free. If you follow my teachings before long you will be able to buy an ox and present it to your master in place of yourself."

Within a short time, slavery had just about become a thing of the past in our Bunjei mission area.

Occasionally at one of the local cattle shows you can see what this new-found freedom means to these people. Once in a while there will appear in the arena a former slave who has been able to pay his ransom with an ox and is now a free man. He is turned loose and dances his head off. Then everyone rejoices with him, all the people clap their hands, shouting, "Tu-a-pa-ndu-la" — "Thank you." It is one of the most moving sights I have ever seen.

The people had to be helped to help themselves. When they found they could, then the slaveowners had no more power over them.

The life that was a combination of serfdom and periodic famine has now been lifted off the backs of the naturally happy and childlike people.

Yet in a way they are still in bondage — a bondage

caused by the darkness in which they live. They can be led out of this too, but as was the case in my experience with slavery, one has to see why they have got themselves into the position they are in, before any of their troubles can be unraveled and they can be led to a higher plane. Above all, the Africans have to be given an incentive, but if one is alert to their ways and knows enough of their language to talk to them, that is not hard to find.

I began to work my way into the Africans' confidence gradually. When I came back to the United States in 1929, I got 11 plows and 60 shovels. The late Mrs. John Hicks and her daughter Gladys gave me $200 for these plows, and the shovels were the first gifts of Boston's Old South Church. Also we started making hoes that were far superior to any ever used by the villagers before. These made it easier to break the river-bottom grasslands. Today there are at least 500 shovels in the area covered by our mission and 75 plows, some of which were imported. Others were made on a simple pattern in our own machine shop.

There are two kinds of African hoe — one for the women which has two short handles in the shape of a V and one for the men which has a single sturdy handle. Neither of these has the leverage of our long-handled American hoe.

The mission today is still lending out plows to men who will bring their oxen to us for training. We have made available to the natives thousands of improved hoes and we have at hand about six oxcarts.

The people told me my hoe was "sacred." When I asked them what they meant, they said it had a lot of

good food in it. They saw the advantage over theirs right
away.

Soon after my arrival I had talked to the native men
about the use of the plow. Their first reaction was, "Mr.
Coles, we don't know how to train the oxen nor have we
any plows or ox-pull chains." When, several years later,
I returned from America with the plows I called in the
men who had oxen and told them a story. I said I would
make the ox-pull chains, yokes and bows and train the
oxen and teach the boys how to plow. Then I would loan
them the use of a plow for a year.

In 1939 I designed and made a plow that could do the
work of twenty to twenty-five men. I made it for $4 or
$5. We sold our plows to the natives about sixty per cent
below what they had to pay at the regular trading centers.

I shall long remember the first man who brought in his
oxen to the mission for training. His name was Sekulu
Chiwaile. He lived at the mountain of Chimbualundu
(Butterfly Mountain). I had told the people that a man
with a plow could do as much work per day as fifteen
could do with a hoe. When Sekulu agreed to bring his
oxen in to be trained, I promised him that he would soon
be getting as high as 50 cents (or 10 angolares) a day for
his team's work. As it turned out, there were dozens of
men waiting to get Sekulu and his plow and oxen to work
for them, and he soon raised his price. He told the people
they would have to pay more so he could get someone to
graze the oxen every day, and could not only get his food
but some salt to go with it.

It was not long before one of the tribal chiefs, Chief
Batata, in the village of Gongo, saw how successful this

plow business was and he brought in four oxen to be trained. In addition to training them, we made the yoke, bows and chains and loaned him the use of a plow for a year. When the year was up the plow was handed over to someone else, but the man was allowed to keep the yoke, bows and chain. The third to catch the spirit and value of the plow was Sekulu Vilenga of the village of Ndala of Sambo. He not only brought his oxen but sent along two boys to be shown how to handle them and to plow.

There are certain rats the Ovimbundu people eat just as some of us did on the farm in the South of the United States. When I was a boy, we ate field and sage rats. The Ovimbundu people eat the same family of rats.

Knowing that the people never have much meat to eat, I said to Senhor Paulino Cardoso, one of our student summer-school teachers, that if I were in his place I would kill rats and exchange them for corn with the people in the villages. Then he could sell the corn and buy an ox. I told him he could fatten up the ox, then kill him and sell the meat at a profit. Eventually he would have two oxen, then he could get a plow.

Senhor Cardoso passed the idea on to a young man who lived across the Cuvalai River and he carried out my idea. I heard the story about three years later. First he bought a pair of oxen with the proceeds from the rats. Then he got a plow. Then he worked hard and grew corn and beans enough to buy a wagon from a Portuguese trader, for which he paid $400. This goes to show how an idea can develop and flower when it is planted at the right time and with the right person. People, when they are

ready and willing, can do a lot to help themselves. I have
seen that proved in Africa.

Today our influences stretch out over thousands of
villages in West Central Africa. Many of our people today own their own plows and oxen. One or two have
oxcarts of their own and nearly every man has a bicycle.
Before we came and began to teach the people how to
farm more efficiently, many of the natives had never
tasted a grain of sugar. Today they buy it in sacks.
There are even a few of our men who are able to take
their wives and children to the coast for vacations. The
plow is fast becoming a "must" piece of farm equipment
in the agricultural life of these rural people.

In 1928 I wrote home: "If it is the will of the Master for
me to stay here another ten years, I hope to see a million
oxen bow their heads to the yoke." You can see what en-
thusiasm we had there at the Galangue mission.

Along about 1938 the Portuguese Governor General
of Angola visited a neighboring county to Galangue where
I had lent a Christian leader the first plow in the county.
In his honor the local Portuguese official had a display of all
the plows and oxen in the county. One man had done so
well he had two plows and oxen enough for both. When
the Governor General saw that achievement he was so
pleased he told the local official to build this man a nice
brick house and furnish him another plow and pair of oxen,
as a reward.

All the sermons preached in that county for the next two
months were on the biblical theme: "To him that hath,
shall be given."

In November of 1950, almost thirty years after my ar-

rival, I was returning one afternoon to Galangue from
Dondi where my wife was in the hospital. I was pushing
my bicycle up hill when I met some men. We started
talking about farming, especially about the cultivation of
wheat, because we were in a valley where the natives had
been cutting and threshing that crop.

As I looked around over these golden fields, I recalled
that when I first came to the colony those valleys now rich
with wheat had been full of wild animals. While we were
talking along this line, a man came along pushing a brand-
new Sunbeam English bicycle. I asked him where he got
that fine bicycle. He smiled and said: "Oh, Mr. Coles
gave it to me."

I asked him what he meant. He said: "It's like this. Mr.
Coles is in Galangue. He's teaching the people how to plant
wheat. When I heard about it I was inspired to go to the
government officials and ask for some seeds to plant myself. When the wheat got ripe, I cut and threshed it.
When I took it to the traders I found I had enough to pay
my taxes, to buy some clothing, and finally this bike. That
is how Mr. Coles gave me the bike."

Intrigued by his story, I asked if he had ever seen Mr.
Coles. He said he had not. "Well," I said, "I am Mr. Coles."
He was dumfounded for a moment. Then overjoyed that
he had seen me "with his own eyes."

By that time, growing wheat had become so vitally important in the minds of the Angola natives that some would
go to heroic extremes to procure their tools. One day a
young man came in to my machine-shop with an all-steel
plow on his shoulders. He dropped his bundle in front of

us, untied it and said he wanted us to assemble the plow
for him. I asked him where he got it. He said: "I bought
it in Johannesburg."

"What," I exclaimed, "you went to Johannesburg just
to get a plow. You mean you carried it on your shoulders
fifteen hundred miles?"

He said: "I did because I had no other way of getting
money enough to buy a plow in Angola."

Not everyone sticks to farming, however. It is not
uncommon for young men from Angola to walk halfway
down the African Continent to earn money to buy a
portable sewing machine, a Victrola or a bicycle. Though
they heard me tell the boys the value of the plow and
had seen its good effects, some of them felt they could
not make money fast enough in Angola to buy the things
they want.

When I read of the congested conditions and racial
friction in Johannesburg today, I come to the conclusion
that it is a reflection on us missionaries. We have not done
enough toward training the Africans to find employment
in their villages and among themselves.

If we as missionaries would go all out to teach Africans
how to develop the things they have in the lands and
around them, we could gradually eliminate these congested areas in the cities and stop communism in its tracks.
You cannot tell me that people who are by nature pastoral
are happy begging at the back door of the white man's
cities.

One day I went about three-hundred miles due north
of Galangue to a place called Gandu to take a truckload

of furniture to a local official. There was the river Gandu
to be crossed. When I got there some men were fixing a
barge which was to take our truck over. While I talked
to the head men, I started giving out some buckwheat
seeds I had, explaining to the people how to plant them
and prepare the grain to eat. I asked one of the men if
he knew who I was. He said he did not. I introduced myself as Senhor Coles of the Bunjei mission of Galangue.

I was much touched by his reply: "Do you mean to tell
me," he asked, "that you are the one I have heard so much
about — the one who has a large house yet will not be
carried on the shoulders of men and who gives himself
freely to us and is still well received by the whites? Are
you that man?"

I had to confess I was.

This was evidence that the news of those little things
I was doing in Galangue for the people traveled much
faster than the words of my sermons. I think they have
had about the same beneficial effect upon the people as a
whole.

Today, whenever I go into a village in Angola where I
am not known by sight, the children and women run
frightened into the bush but as soon as I say I am "Nala
Ko" — that is, Mr. Coles in their language — they come
back happily shouting, "The guest has come — Ukombe
weya!"

Together, I, a humble blacksmith-missionary, and these
Africans who want the word of God translated into a
better life for themselves and their children have come
quite a way.

4

Blessed Are the Meek

THE MASTER once said to his would-be followers: "No man, having put his hand to the plough, and looking back, is fit for the kingdom of Heaven."

Sometimes the obstacles encountered in our efforts to help the Africans have been so big one could not help but feel like turning back.

There was the time, for instance, when we came back in 1936 from our eighteen-month stay in Liberia and found the country all around Galangue plagued by locusts. In Africa they say that everything has its own individual pest, but this was one that had gobbled up everything.

We arrived back at the mission about three o'clock one afternoon in a thirdhand Model A pickup Ford we had bought in Lobito. There was a welcome for us such as I had never witnessed before. I heard them saying over and over to themselves, "Food has come." There was certainly hope and joy in the faces of our Galangue friends that day.

When I surveyed the neighboring field I soon realized

why. The locusts had been there. Every green thing had been stripped bare. The orchards had been killed. Corn and wheat stalks were gnawed right down into the ground.

The locusts arrived in hordes two miles long and half a mile wide. When they had passed, everything in their path was gone. The people had dropped completely the planting of wheat. Livestock had all died, and the lions were encroaching on the traders' settlements.

When the locusts came along in a reddish cloud, the sun went into an eclipse. It was an awesome sight to behold.

The natives were discouraged. They looked to me to find a way out. I held my head in my hands for a while and began to think. Many people around Galangue were on the verge of starvation. How could a man, single-handed, do all that was needed?

Our first job was to kill the locusts. We sent spotters out to spot the locusts as they went into incubation. They located them by following the hawks which went to eat them while they were crawling. They sent word to the village and we went with hundreds of men and killed them by the ton. We wiped out hordes of them like that. At night when it was cold they slept in big piles. We would come across one or two hundred pounds of them hovering together around dry grass and bushes. We took bushes and, starting in at daylight, flayed them until we had killed them before it was warm enough for them to start crawling. This way we saved probably thirty to forty tons of wheat in the area that would otherwise have been devoured.

The Bible speaks of the people in olden times eating locusts and honey. The Africans ate the locusts, preparing them by scalding and pulling the stomachs out. Sometimes they fried them. But alas there was no honey. The locusts had eaten all the flowers and the bees having nothing to feed on had died.

I knew from earlier experience that there were a few plants that the locusts would not eat — chiefly English peas, sweet potatoes and buckwheat. So I immediately arranged for seeds of these and we started planting them in the lowlands. Buckwheat was a new discovery for many of the natives. They liked it because they found that when the hens ate buckwheat they laid more. Buckwheat in Africa gets ripe in six weeks' time after it has been planted. The leaves, the natives discovered, made excellent relish to eat with their mush, so they felt well served.

There were a few energetic men who had their fields planted in manioc, but because so many were on the verge of starvation, they had to stand guard both day and night to keep the people from stealing their produce. I was reminded of my opening sermon at Galangue when Cahamula had stood up and reminded me: "Where there is hunger people do not hesitate to lie and steal." I saw that all my preaching of Christian principles would go for nought if these men were reduced to their animal instincts by the imminence of starvation.

Two men were killed in the fields. Thieves slipped up and shot arrows through their bodies while they were keeping guard. When the news got to me I went to the local officials and asked for native policemen to guard their fields. But we were able to catch only one poor old woman.

I told the people that if they were caught lurking in the bush near the good fields I would take them to the local officials where they would be duly punished. But after two weeks of this waiting and watching, the situation did not ease. I decided then to go to the local chief and talk over some methods that might give better results. When I returned I called the men together and announced my plan. All of the men and boys of Galangue were to be notified that they were to proceed to prepare the land in the valleys for planting. Those who failed to report for this work were to be sent to the local official where they would be given a good beating on their hands, Portuguese style. When I announced this plan, my wife and Mrs. F. S. Dart, who was visiting us, criticized me roundly. They said this was slavery.

"If you call it slavery to make a man work for himself in order that he may keep alive, then I believe in it," I said in a quiet tone.

The results were marvelous. We did not have to send a single man to the officials and after the harvest both the native chiefs came to me saying: "Mr. Coles, you have cured our country."

As the natives gradually became encouraged again, more and more wheat was planted, and the locusts, praise God, began to destroy themselves. When they found less and less to feed on, they turned and destroyed each other.

As I have said before, one of the biggest obstacles in dealing with the African native is his inertia, but the more you get to know the people intimately the more you know what to do about it. Often it is due to some superstition but to get rid of this takes patience and understanding. The natives at first were afraid to sow foreign seeds lest their crops be blasted and famine ensue. And the uninstructed were afraid to plant a fruit tree lest the planter die before the fruit appear.

Little by little we had gained the people's confidence. This, let me say, can only be done by wholehearted genuine participation with them, fitting into their environment when you are their guest and making them feel at home in your environment. This is the great secret, it seems to me, to all success in so-called Point IV work.

Another big obstacle could have come from people who were jealous of our work for one reason or another, but I am happy to say that troubles from this cause in Galangue have been remarkably small. We like to think it is because we have succeeded to an extent in following the exhortation of the Master to love our enemies. This can work wonders, as we have proved.

The Angola land law is that land is pretty much where you find it. The government tries to help the natives own and cultivate land. In 1927, for instance, a law was passed allowing the natives an area five times that which they were actually occupying, but land left uncultivated for more than a year would be regarded as vacant and would then revert to the state. In the case of foreigners, the requirement is that you must cultivate the land for five to ten years with an advertised intention to keep it. Then if no one comes along to claim it, it is yours.

We had established one of our extension schools in the Elombo valley on this basis.

We had some outstanding boys at the Elombo farm. At least they got their start in education and clothing at the farm. One of our boys there passed the grammar school exam and was made a full-fledged grammar school teacher. Another young man, Abraham, was chosen by the mission to go to Dondi to study theology.

The story of a third boy, Chiwumbu, is really impressive. He was a big, strapping member of the Gonguela tribe. His people still wore bark cloth. When he came to me wanting to go to school, he had on a bark cloth. He was an awkward, bashful fellow. We took him in at Elombo, and furnished him with a Bible, hymnbook, syllabus, plate, a bowl and a spoon, slate pencil, blanket, hoe and shovel, and two yards of cloth. That constituted a boy's equipment at Elombo.

The boys at the farm worked every day until four o'clock. Then they cleaned up, ate and had classes until nine. At the end of each year, they took an examination that consisted of reading simple Portuguese, simple addition and subtraction, counting and a little Bible. Those who passed the examination were admitted to the mission school. There they received two shirts, two pair of trousers, coat, blanket, school equipment and tuition, and those boys who were old enough had their taxes paid for them. Chiwumbu was one for whom we had to pay taxes.

Being of a different tribe he had to learn both Portuguese and Umbundu, so he did not move ahead as rapidly as some others. Chiwumbu struggled along in our fifth grade and then got married and went back to his village. For many years Dr. McDowell had been laboring with people of that village trying to get some established work going there but he was not able to do it because he had to use people from the Ovimbundu tribe, who were their enemies.

When Chiwumbu went home, not only with a speaking and working knowledge of Portuguese but with the outlook of a sincere Christian, he started leading groups and was soon not only teaching his people the word of God but was lifting them economically. He soon became an outstanding leader of his village.

When you go there today, you find not only a nice little adobe church with tile roof, but a dozen other branch churches and schools being operated under this mother church. The Gonguela people have abandoned their bark clothes. They are dressing well and tax money is not a nightmare any longer because they are beginning to use plows and plant wheat. The whole community has been put on a sure foundation by this overgrown, zealous young man, Chiwumbu.

Our Elombo school had been founded in 1926 and had been going about seven years. It was a night school preparing boys for the regular mission school. In the daytime they worked in the fields. These boys were part of my special charge and many was the night I had walked those twelve miles from our mission station just to see them.

When trouble struck we had over one hundred boys there. The school and farm were flourishing.

One day a local official (the *chefe*) came along and had us dispossessed. I tried in vain to explain to him that I had been told that because no one before us had been cultivating it, I did not have to register the farm.

At the time he decided to oust us we had lush crops

growing there. Perhaps they aroused his envy. Anyway, we had 141 acres of corn planted. We had 61 acres broken and disked ready to be planted in corn. In another place we had 30 acres of land broken and disked, ready to be planted in rice.

Our hearts were broken when we were told we would have to give it up, after all that work. It hardly seemed possible. But when the local official sent men in to cultivate the corn and beans we had planted, and ordered the land given over to the natives of the villages of Bunjei and Sakalombo, it looked as if misfortune was ours.

As it happened, at the mission at that time Dr. McDowell was engaged in translating the Beatitudes into the Umbundu language. As we talked over the situation, we seemed to hear behind us the words of the Master: "Blessed are the meek: for they shall inherit the earth."

What was there for us to do but to practice the Master's gentleness of spirit?

About that time, the news of the local official's confiscation reached the leading traders in Galangue and Nova Lisboa. They were interested in our village people prospering so they would trade in their posts. They were angry indeed at the local official who had taken our land. They told us we should have taken the matter to court.

Then one day a young man came, saying he was sent by the Bishop of the Catholic Church to tell me that the Bishop was not pleased with the local official's behavior.

After that, the Bishop went to the governor of the district in person to complain about what had been done to us.

We knew how much corn the local official was taking

from the Elombo farm, because when it was ripe and taken to the county seat to this official, our trader friends asked each man how much he had in his sack. They kept track by placing a grain of corn in a bottle.

The first Sunday in April the erring official's baby boy was to be christened by the Bishop of the Catholic Church in the august presence of the governor of the district and all his cabinet members. Right in the middle of the holy affair, the Portuguese Secretary of Agriculture got up and said, "Men, there is something I want to say to you. It is this — the Portuguese government cannot afford to take a few thousands of dollars from our neighbors at the Bunjei mission. Tens of thousands of dollars worth of scorn would be heaped on our heads. The corn must go back!"

The following morning I received a note from the chefe calling me to him. When I got there he told me: "You are to receive all the corn that is left in the field and what I have here." Altogether we received six hundred bushels, probably about one tenth of what had been harvested from our plantings. That was better than nothing, but the loss was a great blow to us. Still we were thankful for the basis of cordial good will that was laid with both the Portuguese and the Catholic missionaries at that time.

Right after the christening, the local official asked the governor to allow him to be transferred. His request was immediately granted and the following Monday morning, for the price of the gasoline only, Dr. McDowell and I did our Christian duty of transporting him far away — to Gandu which is about 350 miles from our place.

Our loss was the Bunjei and Salakambo natives' gain.

Today you go to the Elombo valley in the summer and you will see a rich area about seven miles long and three-hundred yards wide just full of corn. Later on in the fall you will see that same valley full of wheat. And if you peek in the trading houses around there you can see dozens of bicycles in stock waiting to be sold to the natives who will bring in the wheat.

The colonial officers have been very friendly with us. They often spoke of the dwindling delinquency in our area and the local officials looked to our extension workers as real economic leaders in the area. Each of our farm teachers had to go to the Portuguese chefe for a permit, but many of these were granted without examination. We in turn kept our fingers clean and if there was any injustice caused us either by the Catholic Church or any of the traders, the Portuguese always stood ready to rectify it for us.

I made a point of always seeing our local Portuguese official about once a week to talk over my farm plans. Then when necessary I could call on him for credit. A real reciprocity developed. We bought the Portuguese's logs and sold him tiles for his roof. We also took him free in our hospital and furnished him rides when he had to make a long trip. There was much the kind of spirit between us that develops in any frontier community.

It was these small traders who were our neighbors who tried to sell our extension service plan to the big traders and the Portuguese government.

One day in 1937 the Portuguese Corn Exchange in our area received an order from the Canary Islands to produce a large tonnage of special yellow flint corn which was grown only by the Gonguela people way in the interior of Angola. The Exchange looked at the order and realized it could not be filled at a profit because the cost of trucking would be higher than the price they wanted to pay.

So the president of the Corn Exchange and our local chefe came to talk the matter over with me. They wanted me to help them out. They stated their proposition, and I gave them my terms. I told them that if they would give me the corn they wanted planted, pay the salaries of two of my extension workers and pay for my gasoline (gasoline is 60 cents a gallon in Galangue), I would undertake the job. They gave me and the chefe sixty-two short tons of this yellow corn for distribution as seed.

The old men from the village were called in and told they would be paid a premium price for this corn. It was not difficult to get them interested. In fact, the undertaking went over so well that when the crop was in, the member of the Corn Exchange came back and asked me to work out with the chefe an extension service program that would embrace twelve counties. We worked it out. I told them they would need to pay the salaries of twelve young men to act as extension agents, and to subsidize the making of yokes, bows and chains, and the training of the oxen. Then we would need 10 tons of corn, 10 of wheat and 10 of beans to be distributed among the people. I said we would need 500 plows and 500 shovels for loan to the African farmers.

The program was sent to Portugal for ratification by the Secretary of the Colonies. He wrote back to the Corn

Exchange official: "Men, you have a fine program but you are outside your sphere. You are there only to buy corn. The growing of it falls under the Department of Agriculture."

That was all we heard until two years later when word was received from Lisbon that an Agricultural Extension Department was to be established in Angola with headquarters in Nova Lisboa. The government sent there three well-trained and educated Portuguese agricultural extension directors. That year the government distributed 1060 tons of corn and about 600 tons of wheat to the natives at the proper planting season. Instead of loaning plows to the natives as I had planned to do, they sold 2700 to them at cost price.

From 1939 until this day, the Portuguese government is distributing thousands of tons of seeds to the natives and many of the large trading houses have started importing plows. At first some were sold at a high price but the government soon put clamps on the traders.

The benefits of this program that is helping the people to help themselves cannot be measured in dollars and cents, but I feel safe in saying that the economic life of the colony has increased 150 per cent or more. I like to think that we at Galangue were the spark plug for that forward-looking program that is doing so much for the people of Angola, making them self-sufficient in a field that is most natural to them — agriculture.

This economic progress has added to the work of our Protestant and Catholic missions. They cannot furnish enough education today. Each year they raise their tuition

but the next year a new line has formed at the door waiting for an education. The natives for the first time are
able to pay tuition because they are the proud owners of
flourishing fields of wheat, corn and beans.

Since Portugal is a Catholic country, we Protestants
might have run into considerable difficulty with our missions but we were always careful to avoid this kind of
trouble. We felt it very important not to let bitter sec-
tarianism mar the united Christian front with which we
were trying to convert the Africans. We would not get
very far in our work if we preached "Love your neigh-
bor," but did not practice that demand of the Master.

Our relations with the Catholic missions in our area
were always cordial. At Galangue we were always careful
not to speak against them. When I was traveling in the
neighborhood of their missions, I always made a point of
going there to spend the night. When I was invited to
mass, I attended. The Catholic missions all had excellent
demonstration farms, better than we had at Galangue, and
of course they interested me, since that was my special field
of work.

It was because of my Point IV work that the Catholics
at one stage asked me if I would help them develop the
Cunene Basin in the Quanyama country. But when I
visited there in August 1938, I spent the night at the
Catholic mission of Mupa and was frankly told by the
director that he did not want outside interference, and
despite official support for my work there, he was going to
do all he could to keep us Protestants out of the Quanyama
country. He even had the Catholic Bishop come down

so he could put the case before him. The Portuguese officials were on our side since they were the ones who had first invited us, but temporarily, at least, the local director won out, and I left the Cunene Basin without having been able to help any of the people.

After I had worked and waited for eight years, however, the Master opened the door for us, and when I returned to the area in 1946 accompanied by a trained nurse for lepers and two young men to make butter and cheese and with plans to establish a school, and put in a system of wells, I found a letter from the governor to the administrator saying that we could start work in any part of Quanyama we wished. He said further that our teachers did not have to take the government examination, nor did we have to build the first-class school buildings that were usually required. What we had done in Galangue spoke for itself, in the increased prosperity of the region, and so the Catholic Church's opposition to our plans for helping Quanyama were gradually overcome.

The people of Quanyama were badly in need of better houses. Their huts were built so a man couldn't even step into his own house in an upright position. To keep such hovels clean was out of the question. The old men talked the way people usually do when they are not interested in seeing things made better. They said God didn't want them to have better houses.

In that area there were men who owned ten thousand head of cattle, yet they were doing practically nothing with the milk. You needed a gas mask to eat their butter. We wanted to help them make it palatable, so it would be a good commercial product.

One of the recommendations I made was that the Administration put in wells. This area borders on the extensive Kalahari Desert and the people need water, not only so they can irrigate their crops, but so they won't have to travel miles just to get water to drink or to use for refrigerating their dairy products. During the dry season, the people had to go forty to fifty miles to the Cunene River to get water for themselves and their cattle. Yet I knew there was water, close to the surface. You could tell by the fossils and other signs that ten to fifteen feet down there would be nice clean water. Later I was told by the Portuguese administration that eighteen experimental wells had been dug and fifteen had produced sparkling water.

Another experiment I recommended during my Quanyama visit was the planting of rice. Looking around, I saw a lot of good land going to waste. There were thousands of acres of open land that would hold lakes of water during the rainy season. Then during the dry season, the water would disappear. I was sure, from my rice-planting experiments in Galangue, that it would make good rice land. Then, in dry periods, it could be used for wheat.

I promised when I got back to Galangue to send the English officials (part of Quanyama is under British control, the rest of it Portuguese) some rice, also some wheat and a plow. I sent them about a bushel of rice through the Extension Department and when I last heard, they had planted it and it was growing, marking what I hope will be the start of a new life for those African natives. I went back there in 1947 and rice was on the way to becoming one of the staple crops of Ovamboland and the entire Quanyama country.

Their great lack at that point was a hulling machine. I still hope to be able to help them with this some day.

The Quanyama country is in the southern part of Angola and borders on the Kalahari Desert on the south. Its northwest border is the Cunene River. From the Quanyama country to Nova Lisboa, which is on the railroad, is over four hundred miles. Such farm produce as corn and beans cannot be hauled that distance by trucks at a profit. So the natives cultivate only what they need for their personal needs. But the plow has entered that faraway country from the Portuguese side. It came about in this way. A young man from the Quanyama country came to our mission station. He attended school for three years and during that time learned to plow and drive oxen. He went home with new knowledge of farming, and with the word of God burning in his heart to help his fellow men. Though his first job was as an interpreter at the county seat, he knew the value of the plow so he bought one. Immediately he went up in the respect of the people round about.

At that time in Quanyama the price of an ox ranged from a dozen strings of beads, or a wife, to four or five dollars. But when the people began to see the real value of an ox, the price jumped almost overnight to $20 or $25.

We Negroes have a saying: "There are always more ways of killing a dog than choking him with butter." That means that if things are really crying out to be done as they are in Africa, then if one is persistent and patient and has "cast his net on the right side," he will always find a way over or around the obstacles in his path.

5

God Takes Care of Fools and Babes

WHEN MY WIFE and I took charge of the medical work at the Galangue mission in 1923, I guess we were the fools and the poor sick Africans were the babes.

She had had just a year's training in nursing at Talladega College Hospital in Alabama. I had had thirteen months in the medical branch of the United States Army in France.

I had taken with me to Portuguese West Africa an army medical manual and Bertha had packed in our baggage several books on nursing. One of these — a book of 1700 pages — proved over the years to be worth its weight in gold (*Health and Longevity*, by Joseph G. Richardson).

Usually when an African calls in a medical doctor, he has already tried the native witch doctor. Although the witch doctors in our area knew that I did not approve the show they put on in diagnosing a case, they knew they had my continuing sympathy for the work they were doing and as a result relations between us were good. There is no doubt that witch doctors seem to cure some cases that baffle doctors but the basis of their work is fear and in these modern days many natives are beginning to repudiate the old superstitions on which the practices are founded.

The African witch doctor presents an awesome picture, with his startling regalia and eerie equipment. He may have a crown made from the mane of a lion with bright-colored feathers in it. Perhaps he wears a necklace made of the skin of a python. On it may be tied the claws of a lion, and on his arms will be bracelets made of copper with beautiful figures carved on them and some made from the skins of animals he has killed. Over his shoulder is slung the horn of a deer which he blows to summon the spirits to reveal things to him.

The witch doctors tell the people that death is caused by spirits. Then they try to help the sick people to find out just which spirit is causing the trouble so that the culprit can be appeased by sacrifice.

His equipment consists of all the trinkets he can get into a basket about four inches deep and six or seven inches in diameter. Chief among these is an image carved in the shape of a man whose name is Chimbanda. Chimbanda was the first doctor who lived on earth. He died at the beginning of time but his spirit lives in the heavens. Only those who know the languages of the spirits can communicate with Chimbanda.

It is an impressive sight to see a witch doctor diagnosing a case. He may have three or four muffled drums pounding and several other musical instruments throbbing, and a group of men and women chanting in a low doleful tone of voice. Against this mournful background, the witch doctor talks to the image — Chimbanda — in a strange tongue, who sends the message on to the heavens and gets one in return.

When the message is received, if it is good, the witch doctor jumps up and down kicking, runs around and blows his deer horn.

Besides the image of Chimbanda, the witch doctor's basket contains a variety of small items, including the neck of a small gourd, the foot of a chicken, the horn of a goat, or a piece of a horn of an ox, or the hoof of a pig, buttons, cloth pins, and so forth.

As the witch doctor talks to the image in the basket he keeps the basket in motion so the trinkets will move about and come in contact with the image. By the witch doctor's clever manipulation, the image is brought into contact with just the right object which the spirit in the heavens wants the witch doctor and his co-workers to have as their fee.

If the image comes into contact with the gourd first, it means that the spirit wants the men to have some strong beer before any remedies for the illness will be revealed. So the friends and relatives of the sick person will go and make the beer. Probably it will take two days to brew it and in the interim the poor man may die, but they are all convinced that while the men are drinking, the spirit of the first medicine man is getting his share and when he has had it, he will speak again.

This time he tells what the sick man is to pay the witch doctor for the treatment.

If the sick man has plenty of cattle, the image is going to

throw itself on the ox's horn and stay with it. The witch doctor will turn and tell the relatives of the sick that Chimbanda wants an ox. Only when they agree to pay, will he "divine" again to find out what drug is to be used.

Forty or fifty years ago African witch doctors used to use the poison test. The doctors knew all the local poisons and they would brew up batches of them. Then they would give them to their patients, telling them if they were innocent of bad deeds, they would vomit up the poison. But if the doctor thought the man was guilty or for some reason didn't want him around any more, he would concoct a real knockout brew. Nowadays, it is not quite so tough to be treated by a native doctor since the biggest penalties are fines.

If the man has lots of cattle, quite likely it will take the witch doctor a long time to cure him. For each treatment he will charge an ox.

Taken as a whole, the witch doctors of Africa represent the intelligentsia of the tribes. They have had many years of schooling and study at the feet of their fathers and uncles who were witch doctors before them. They have a look and a poise which sets them off from the crowd, probably because of the different moods they throw themselves into from time to time. Like great men of the theater, they have balanced carriage and an imposing look at all times.

Once I asked a witch doctor, a friend of mine, why he carried on all the foolishness I have just described. In a moment of frankness he said that if he did not go through with that ritual, the people just would not believe that he had the power to heal.

Perhaps somewhat the same thing is true with us "civilized" people. When we go into a doctor's office and see lots of books and equipment, does not the impression they leave add to our faith that the possessor of them can cure us?

One day in August 1926 I visited a region about twenty miles south of our mission in Galangue, known as Sakalombo. Distant sounds of chanting and dancing lured me as I approached. When I entered the village and inquired what occasioned the celebration, I was told a sick woman was being treated. I was shown the native doctor. He was stripped to the waist and barefooted. His nakedness was interrupted only by a loin cloth, bracelets and a reed buckhorn necklace made from the skin of an eland. A leopard-skin cap, pierced with several kinds of feathers, rested on his head, and in his hand he held several whistles on which he blew every few minutes; on the ground beside him lay an elephant's tail. In his basket I could distinguish an ox's horn, the hoof of a pig, a small gourd for drinking beer, a chicken's foot, and the garbed image of a man. The doctor went through much gyration and incantation as he juggled the trinkets up and down.

About a dozen natives formed a semicircle around the doctor. In their hands they carried gourds filled with small stones, which they rattled as they chanted and clapped hands to the rhythms of the drummers. I was fascinated by the colorful sight and asked to see the sick woman. She was in a house about forty yards away. The doctor sent for her. When she came I examined her, and found she had had a paralytic stroke in her right arm. I told the doctor that he could not cure this woman, as there were only a few doctors in Europe and America who could cure such cases. He insisted that he could do it. I promised to give him four oxen if he could effect this cure, and I went on to Musungo. Several months later I passed through Sakalombo again. I located the witch doctor and asked him how his patient was getting along. He told me she had been cured. I replied, "Ove akasi loku kemba" — "You are lying." Then I asked to see the woman. He sent for her, and I immediately recognized her. Her arm had filled out and she was able to work. I caught her by the arm and pulled it. It was as strong as the other. I had to pay four oxen.

I questioned the doctor about the treatment he had used, and he told me that first he bled the arm, by cutting a hundred or more fine holes with the point of a knife. Then he massaged it until all the black blood there was in it came out. Then he rubbed in some medicine. This was repeated until the blood cleared up and became red. To cover up his story with magic, he said that the arm had to be rubbed after each treatment with ashes made by burning the fangs of a snake with the claws of a lion.

Mungumba was one of the students at our Mission Boarding School. One day she became ill with a dread disease known as *oku lenda*. We had several cases of this disease before, but our medical knowledge did not enable us to effect a cure. The disease usually started with a slight swelling under the eyes, which gradually spread to the face, then started in the legs and moved upward. When it reached the abdomen, diarrhea set in, and that meant death. I treated Mungumba for several weeks, but she showed no signs of improvement. One day her brother came to us and asked if he could take the girl to a native witch doctor in the Guanguela country. Although it was against the rules of our mission to release a patient for treatment by a witch doctor, in this instance we did not object as we knew we could not cure the girl. She was carried away to a distant village, and whenever people from that village came to our mission we inquired about our patient. We were told that she was improving. Several months passed. One day I saw a girl coming toward me down the road, carrying a basket of beans on her head. When she came close she called me by name. I recognized the voice of Mungumba, but not her face. The girl I looked at was as white as any white person I had ever seen. Not only was her skin white, but also her hair and eyelashes. All the pigment in her body had been destroyed. I investigated the method of cure, and the closest I could ascertain was that violent purges had been used, the body had been pricked with a keen knife and bled and various medicines had been rubbed in. The medicines were so strong that they destroyed the pigment of the skin. In 1940, just before I left Angola, I saw Mungumba. She had regained her pigment and with the exception of a few white spots and white eyelashes she was black again.

Dangala, one of the boys at our Mission Boarding School, became ill one day and was taken to the hospital. He grew very thin, and several large blisters appeared on the soles of his feet. He almost lost his mind, and when the boy showed no improvement in several weeks, his people came to the hospital in the dark of the night and stole him out, and took him to a witch doctor. The witch doctor was unable to do anything for him, but there was a young Christian in the same village who said he could cure the boy. He proceeded to bleed him, and it was said that what came out of the boy looked more like milk than blood. The bleeding was kept up for several days and medicine was rubbed in several times a day. He was given three or four purges. Today the boy is a strong and healthy young man. I talked with the man who cured this boy. I asked him how he knew the "bush" so well, though he was not a witch doctor. He told me that whenever he saw a bad case and someone cured it, he paid the healer whatever price he asked to be taught the cure.

The native doctors have a unique way of removing cataracts from eyes. They take a quill and blow into the eye at intervals until the cloudiness goes away.

The African people make excellent patients. They can stand much pain. They are simple and childlike and many will get well without the use of any kind of drugs or herbs.

As far as ritual is concerned, it wasn't long before I had evolved one of my own. Before I learned how to diagnose the local diseases I had to look in my "big book." The people soon found out that I looked in the book first thing. So when a man did not recover as rapidly as he thought he should, he would say in a nice way, "Mr. Coles, I wonder if you have looked in the book?" I always said I had but told him his case was a little harder than some of the others. Then I would say with authority, "But you will soon be well." And I meant it.

I found that many of the people had faith not only in the "book" but in certain drugs. For instance, the color and

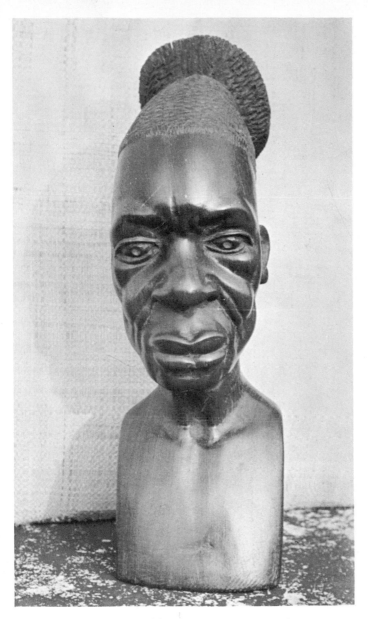

A bust carved in wood — a rare example
of present-day African art

Oxen pulling a log, which will be cut into lumber

Four of the men who learned carpentry and iron-mongering at the mission, working with me on the production of an oxcart

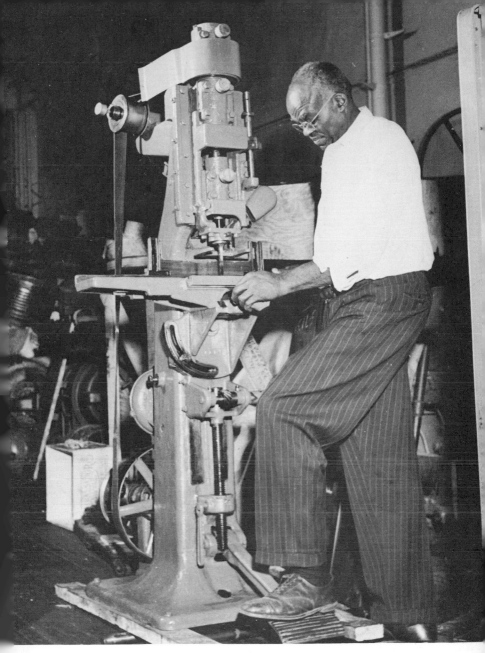

Myself in our machine shop at Galangue. I am working a mortising machine, which will mortise forty to fifty wagon hubs a day. (*Our World Foto*)

These
are among
the iron
and pottery
objects
I learned to
make on one
of my leaves
in the U. S.

The edge of Lobito

The mission hospital.
We made the bricks our-
selves, produced every bit
of the building materials,
right down to the hinges
in the doors, in our own
plant. Only the glass was
imported. I was the
architect.

Myself and fellow worker in a
wheat field, close to harvest time

One of the ox-drawn
plows made in our own shop
at the Mission

The Reverend Jesse Chipenda of Lobito with his family.
He is one of the best farmers in Angola as well as
a preacher held in high regard by natives and
Europeans alike.

taste of a certain drug may become known forty or fifty miles away because it has cured someone. People would tell you what they needed before they were even examined. If you asked them how they knew they needed that special medicine, they would say, "Did it not cure Sekulu Hosi? Am I not sick of the same thing?" If you gave him the medicine he wanted he was almost always well in a few days. I found that when I won the faith and confidence of the natives either in myself or my medicine, eighty per cent of the healing work was accomplished.

The African patient receives everything with a deep sense of gratitude. How many times people I had treated and my wife had fed would come back several months later bringing a chicken or some other present because "you took me out of the grave." This is an *olupandu*, or thank offering.

We had not been in Galangue more than three weeks when there was a sad happening. One of the boys was cut in the head with a hoe by another boy in a tussle in the Joka River valley where they were preparing land for a garden. The cut was about two inches long and went to the skull. Since I had been put in charge of the mission's medical work, they brought the boy to me.

I got everything ready. First I scrubbed the boy's hair. Then I shaved the hair from the cut place and then improvised a needle to sew up the wound. I took a long needle out of Bertha's work basket and pushed each end of it into a cork by main force. Then I heated it in the middle, and bent it into a curve which made it just right to sew up the scalp of the boy's head.

Luckily we had some silk thread. I boiled both it and

the needle, then put them in alcohol while I was cleaning the boy's head. I washed out the cut and around it with a solution containing twenty per cent carbolic acid, then I sponged the place off with alcohol and proceeded to sew it up. I used a wet dressing of Lysol. The place healed.

As a matter of fact, when I took the dressing off, the scar was so light it looked as though it had been made by a briar.

The people crowded around to inspect my medical handiwork and I can tell you when they saw it and learned it had healed in about ten days, my stock went up on the native market.

In the seven years in which I was forced to practice medicine among the Africans, I always asked the Master to direct me in the treatment of those poor benighted people who came to my door as they had to His more than nineteen hundred years ago. When I listened to Him, He always gave me an answer.

As my medical skill advanced over that of the Ochimbanda (witch doctor) my practice grew heavier. I soon was forced to have sick calls twice a day.

My hospital equipment consisted of one room with a camp cot and three light blankets of my wife's. I had no hospital clothing at all, but I had brought along some of those long army undershirts so I used them. Whenever anyone was brought in sick, the first thing I would do would be to clean him up and put a shirt on him. He usually felt better right away. One day Mrs. McDowell said to me, "Coles, you will not have enough shirts for all the people coming to you sick." It occurred to me that she did not want me to be nice to these poor people but I soon discovered that she was speaking the truth.

Soon I had reached the bottom of the trunk those shirts were in and had none left for myself, but at least I had the satisfaction of knowing that I had shared my shirts with those who needed them most.

I will never forget the first pneumonia case I had. I am sorry to say the man died. Before he passed away I learned a humbling lesson about the African mind which has lasted with me ever since. One night when I went to see the man I heard him saying to himself over and over: "Ha. Suku yange ame nda linga nye ngechele" — "My God, what have I done. Forgive me."

Here was a man we thought knew nothing about the God we came from America to tell him of. Yet from his murmurings we knew his god Suku was as real to him as the Christian God was to me. He was praying in his own way.

Up to that time I had been thinking that I could bring God to these natives in my suitcase, but I found him already there, just waiting to be called up.

Although we could not save our first pneumonia case, we were lucky with all the ones that followed. My wife put into practice what she had been taught at Talladega College Hospital about nursing that disease. She would keep some kind of pneumonia jacket on the patient until he was ready to go home.

My practice increased so rapidly that I soon had to have some help. I called in a bright young man to aid me. His name was Daniel Sakalombo Njava. He proved to be a

very fine nurse. Later he went to a Portuguese government hospital for training and became a registered nurse.
He is now working in the Benguela Railroad Hospital of
Nova Lisboa at a salary of about sixty dollars a month,
which is very good pay in Angola.

After Senhor Njava had learned the names of the drugs
and their usage and dosage, he was called Doctor by those
who knew him, but he still had a long way to go to really
earn that title. One evening about six o'clock when I came
in Daniel met me at the door greatly disturbed. He said:
"Chalepa is very sick. She is vomiting lots of blood." I
asked him what he had given her and he replied: "Two
hours ago I gave her a dose of epsom salts. That is all."

I asked him where he got it and he showed me a jar
which was marked plainly "saltpeter" — he had given that
poor girl a soupspoonful of saltpeter.

Mentally I went down on my knees and asked the Master to tell me what to do. I was led to wash out the girl's
stomach and give her a cup of strong tea. Within less than
fifteen minutes we had everything under control again.

As a rule, we gave out quinine in liquid form. For an
adult we gave a soupspoonful.

We had a girl in our home by the name of Chilombo,
who ran the house for us while we were at work in the
mission. She was a student. One day when she was not
feeling so well she decided that she would take a dose of
quinine. We kept as a rule the bulk of drugs in the storeroom of our house. Chilombo knew that we gave a spoonful of quinine as a dose. So she went into the storeroom
and got the package of quinine in powder form. She took

a "heaping spoonful." I was off in the field at the time, repairing a broken harrow. When I looked up there was a young man standing in front of me, completely out of breath. When he finally could speak he said, "Come quickly to the house because Chilombo is very ill." So I dashed for the house as fast as I could go. When I got there Chilombo was on the floor as limp as a dishrag with the other girls standing around her wringing their hands and crying. One of the girls volunteered that Chilombo had taken a large spoonful of quinine in powder form. Again I called on the Master for guidance. He told me to wash out the stomach and give the girl a cupful of olive oil, which I did. We put her in a warm bed and the next morning she was somewhat better and gradually recovered.

Once my head "boy" became constipated. For this our remedy in bad cases was to give a drop of croton oil. Senhor Daniel decided he needed two drops. He took them. That evening he became sick but he did not say why. He grew worse until his eyes were sunken and had a glaring look. Then he admitted he had taken two drops of croton oil. By that time I knew that it would do no good to wash his stomach. Then the "still small voice" told me to get the book and look up antidotes for croton oil. So I got it, leafed through the pages, and sure enough found it. It recommended flaxseed meal. By the grace of God we had five pounds of that. So I made up two ounces of it into a thin gruel and gave it to Daniel to drink. Two hours later I went back to see how he was. I tiptoed in. How relieved I was to find his eyes "unfixed." The Master and I had again triumphed over death.

One day a group of us at Galanague were training an ox. He was tied to a log. Suddenly he dashed off with it. The end flew around and struck a man on the leg so hard it broke it.

My army medical training came in handy then. A Thomas Splint came before my eyes. So I took the measurements of the man's thigh and broken leg. Then I went to the blacksmith shop and got a three eighths inch piece of iron, cut it off according to the measurements, and made a splint. Then I set the bone. When I took the splint off you could feel only a small ridge where the break had knitted together. The man walked thereafter without a limp.

During the early part of our practice a woman came in with a very large stomach. I did not know immediately whether it was a tumor or dropsy and even if I had known, I wouldn't have known what to do.

It was my custom to consult the doctors about the cases which I felt incompetent to handle. So I sent word to Dr. Fred S. Stokey, who at the time was at Dondi, the central school of the American and Canadian Boards of Angola, West Africa, and asked him to teach me how to diagnose the two conditions and how to tell the difference between them. He said, "First put your hand on one side of the abdomen with the fingers on it. Then with the other hand hit the abdomen gently. If you get a fluid vibration, it is dropsy. If no vibration, then it is a tumor."

As luck would have it Dr. Stokey came down to spend the weekend with us. The following morning I was holding our regular morning sick call. Among those who were sick was a woman with an unusually large abdomen. I showed her to Dr. Stokey. He said, "All right, Coles. Examine her." I did. I said: "It is a case of dropsy." So on the table she was placed in the open air. Just above the navel we cleansed a place six inches wide, then Dr. Stokey made the small incision in which he inserted a small rubber tube and drained off two quarts of the fluid. Then a bandage was put over the incision. Within a few days the woman was well and able to go about her daily tasks of flailing the meal for her family.

About a week after that a boy of ten or twelve came up looking as though he was about to burst. I examined him. Here I was able to diagnose another case of dropsy. So on the table he was placed. In a few minutes we had taken two and one half quarts of fluid from him. I tapped six different people altogether. I lost only one case, I think by taking out too much fluid which caused the heart to "bleed to death."

I recall very well the last case I tapped. It was a little girl about twelve years old. I had to operate on her four times. Since she was so small, we gave her a little chloroform. Bertha was my anesthetist. She had been told by the doctors that chloroform was hard on the heart, therefore one should be careful in its use. So she didn't administer enough to keep the child well under. The youngster squirmed and twisted so much that suddenly about half a yard of omentum had spewed forth through the incision I had made in the abdomen.

I did not let on to Bertha that I was a little excited at the sight. Instead I told her quietly I thought we had taken out enough. So I pushed the omentum back into the abdomen as quickly as I could, then put a gauze wick in the hole, with a gauze bandage over it. This allowed free drainage.

When the excitement was over, I gave the child a good examination. I discovered that her liver was down over her stomach and as hard as a board. Then I treated her for liver trouble. When it was cleared up, no more fluid accumulated in the body cavity and the child was well.

A doctor is not supposed, according to tradition, to treat members of his family, but I had to do it twice in the African jungle.

When my daughter Laura was a child she ate some native berries that were poisonous. The girl who was caring for her told her not to do it, but she would not listen. That night about twelve o'clock she started vomiting and kept it up about every ten minutes. I looked in the "big book" for the antidote for "vegetable poisoning." It said a drop of carbolic acid in a glass of water would stop the vomiting. I tried it on Laura. Within a short time she went to sleep and did not vomit any more.

When Edward was four years old he was playing and jumping in the carpenter shop. He jumped on a nail, which just about pierced his foot. This was in the middle of the day. Bertha dressed it. I went to the field and when I got back that night about seven o'clock the child was in agony. His foot was swollen up way beyond its normal size.

I understood what that meant so I made ready a probe. I wrapped a piece of gauze around it, then saturated it with a strong solution of iodine. The men held him fast while I pushed the probe through his foot where the end of it could be seen pushing against the outside skin of the foot. I twisted the probe around several times before drawing it out. When we took it out, Bertha put Edward to bed. He soon went to sleep and did not wake up through the night.

Not knowing how the case would come out, early the next morning I jumped on my bicycle and went for Dr. Stokey to Dondi which is ninety-nine miles from Galangue. Impelled by my anxiety, I did it in six hours. Dr. Stokey and I returned in his motorcycle. When we got back we found Edward playing. Dr. Stokey turned to me and said, "You did the right thing. Now I shall tell you how to do it so it will not be so painful to the next patient." He told me to take a syringe needle and cut it off, then fill the syringe full of iodine and inject it into the hole. Praise God, I never had to do it!

One of the favorite African pastimes is the "brush hunt." When the grass is good and dry they set fire to it just before the planting season in order to clear the ground. The blazes leap high. While the grass is burning two or three hundred men will be watching and looking with their bows and arrows in their hands, so when a rabbit or other animal is driven out by the fire, they shoot him. Sometimes they hit a man instead. Men have even been killed by their comrades in this extremely dangerous sport.

During one of these hunts the chief of the Chisitu was caught in between two large clumps of grass. He had a lot of cloth draped around his waist. It reached to his feet, so when the cloth took fire the poor old chief was in a very bad position. He was severely burned from his head to his feet.

His tribe was so isolated that they were two days getting

him to us for treatment. By the time he got to us those places where the skin had sloughed off were full of maggots.

The interesting thing about this particular case was that this man had an advanced case of elephantiasis. The burns took three months to heal, but after they had healed there was not a trace of elephantiasis to be seen. Those who saw it and had the same malady said they were willing to be subjected to the same treatment, but I was doubtful. In order to prevent the chief's legs from being drawn I kept them strapped down on splints. Prayer and medical care and nursing restored him to health.

All of the obstetrical work among the local women was taken care of by my wife, Mrs. McDowell and some of the trained African women. The infant mortality rate in Angola is very high because the women work too long in the damp river bottoms. Once I was called in on a delivery of a Portuguese woman. I found the placenta had been retained. I was afraid to do anything myself but I directed a Portuguese how to take it. I had him take hold at the end and twist it gently, and then little by little pull it out. I examined to see if there were any adhesions. There were none, but I had her cleaned and packed on general principles and soon she was well and about.

For a variety of reasons, native children are subject to many kinds of convulsions. I have seen cases where youngsters did not open their eyes for thirty-six hours. At first I was baffled and did not know how to handle these. But one day something told me to look in "the book" in the section on home remedies. I looked, and first thing I read was that salt in small doses on the tongue is good for convulsions. I tried this simple remedy and within three minutes the child I was treating was looking about normally. When her mother called her, she responded. She had been speechless for many hours. What joy it was to all of us to see the change. It seemed as if the few grains of salt were able to cast out gloom and usher in happiness — but we thanked God, too.

Because of the polluted streams from which the natives get their drinking water, the people suffer greatly from dysentery. Every year at the beginning of the rainy season this disease takes a heavy toll of babies and children. I had to treat a woman for this disease once. I watched her day by day as she wasted away. I had used every drug we had in stock on her with no avail.

As a last resort I looked in the "book" under home remedies. I discovered that kerosene was good for dysentery. So I gave this dear woman, who would probably have been dead in a few more days, a tablespoon of kerosene. Two hours later I went to her to see how she was faring. The minute I looked at her I knew she was better from the expression on her face. When I asked her how she was she said, "Oh, I am well." From then on I used only kerosene to treat dysentery.

There is an ailment in Angola which is found mostly in children. The body and face swell beyond recognition. I regret to say I lost my first two or three cases of this disease, so it was with some trepidation I approached the case of a two-year-old child of Senhor Jongola Malenga who came down with this dreadful disease. I did all I could but the child grew steadily worse. So I told his father to call in a native doctor. One came but when he saw the child he said, "I cannot do a thing to help him." His mother and father had given up all hope for him. Every day they placed him behind the house on a mat and waited for the last. On my return from the field one afternoon I passed the house. Here was the poor little thing on the mat, waiting for death. He looked more like a balloon than a child. Judging from the way he was groaning, I thought the end must be near. In despair, I asked the Master to show me what to do. It was three o'clock in the afternoon. I went to the "book" and traced down everything which came under the heading "dropsy." I came across "peritonitis dropsy" whose symptoms seemed to be those of the child. The treatment was given; namely, sulphuric acid, quinine, iron, strychnine and bichloride of mercury. When Bertha heard that she yelled out, "Oh, don't give that child that. If you do, you will kill him." I said, "If he dies I will never feel that what I gave him was the cause."

So I took a pinch of this and a nip of that and put them in a pint of water and mixed them well. Every four hours I gave the little fellow a tablespoon full of it. After eight days of treatment he was on the road to recovery and ready to go home.

The news of this so-called "miraculous" cure was soon known in many parts of the country round about. So people soon started bringing their children in from far and near for treatment.

Dr. Walter S. Strangway of Chissamba, a Canadian who is stationed at their mission station of Chissamba, which is

250 miles northwest of us, came to spend the weekend with us. While he was there, two girls from the same village came in with their faces beginning to swell. I asked Strangway to prescribe for them. He said, "Coles, if you tell me what you prescribe I will tell you." I said, "Well, I will discharge them within eight days." At the expiration of that time they were on their way home.

In September of 1931 Dr. Aaron M. MacMillan came to Galangue after spending eighteen months in Portugal where he studied and completed the work for his medical degree in Portuguese. He took over the medical work of the Galangue mission station. He soon proved to be a credit not only to the Negro race in the field of medicine but to a nation. His name will go down in history as one of the outstanding doctors of Angola during his time.

Having to train all of his medical assistants and nurses, he asked me to help him with operative cases and I became his anesthetist. I worked with him in this capacity for three years. We did not let a single patient die on the operating table. And Dr. MacMillan performed all types of operations that could be performed on the human anatomy.

Here was a case of a better mouse trap. It must have been, because there were both Europeans and Africans from all parts of Angola in the Willis F. Pierce Memorial Hospital for all kinds of treatments. It was all right for Dr. MacMillan to be a good doctor, yes, even a good surgeon, but the amazing thing to me about his work was that he was not afraid to undertake and perform an operation on any part of the human body with African young men and women who were trained under him. Although his European practice was very heavy, there were a hundred or more African patients in and around the hospital at all times. He might do an operation upon a European for $200 and turn around and perform the same operation upon an African for nothing. Never did he have a trained nurse from America or Europe to help him. Yet his medical work was of the same standard and quality as of any hospital in Angola.

MacMillan's experience proves to me that the Africans are able to grasp anything one really tries to teach them.

One of the great nurses at Galangue was Mrs. Nachilulu Jololo. She had never been able to get out of the second grade in the Portuguese schools. Since my wife had charge of the mission school, she turned the care of our home over to Mrs. Jololo. When Dr. MacMillan came he said to Bertha: "I will need the best and most dependable girl or woman you have on the place as my nurse." Bertha hated to give Mrs. Jololo up but she knew she would have to. Having had some nursing training herself, she knew the doctor needed someone he could train and trust. So Mrs. Jololo was turned over to the hospital to be trained as a nurse. When she was in school, she never did study Portuguese, but after six months in the hospital she was speaking it as well as any of the other boys and girls in training. Mrs. MacMillan had a class in chemistry; the young men and women who were taking the course had finished at our station school as well as our central training school of Dondi. When it came time for the examinations, Mrs. MacMillan always let someone else do Nurse Jololo's writing for her. The nurse dictated her answers and at times made marks higher than half or more of the class. Dr. Mac-Millan said unqualifiedly she was the best nurse he had ever had, in America or Europe.

The Portuguese government maintains hospitals and health centers in the cities of Angola and in some of the outlying areas for treatment of Africans. There are hospitals with some outstanding native doctors who give themselves to the treatment and training of the natives, but in the light of needs of the whole colony, the picture today is still very dark. Almost all mission stations as a rule have hospitals and give some training to the native young men and women, but it is far from enough.

For ailments affecting eyes, nose, throat, ears and teeth, there is no provision in the whole setup for the "bush" native. Those who can pay the price can go to a Portuguese specialist. But how many Africans are there who have the money for such treatment? The same is true of dental work. There is not a place in Angola where a native can go to have a tooth filled.

You can see how sadly the African needs the help in this field of trained outsiders really interested in his welfare.

6

How an African Thinks

ANY MAN who goes to Africa thinking he is the first to introduce an idea of God to the natives is in for a letdown. Once he has learned the language and is able to talk with and work close to the people, he will learn some amazing things about them and the way they think.

When I heard the dying man praying to Suku for forgiveness, it came to me then and there that these people I was to work with thirty years had a natural concept of good and evil behavior and a belief that there was a Being outside oneself who was able to punish for evil-doing but to whom one could come and ask forgiveness. That man had never heard a missionary preach and had never been to church, but as I said, he knew about God.

Often since then I have heard little children say, when they have been accused of something they did not do: "Suku, eye ombange yange; ame, sackilingile" — "God is my witness; He knows I did not do it." But when he is guilty and he knows you know it, he will say: "Ngechele; ame si chi lingi vaili" — "Forgive me; I will not do it again."

Again the thought of God as a Supreme Being is inherent in children's attitude toward pardon. If an African has harmed you he will ask you to pardon him, but if he has committed a sin which he thinks is displeasing in the sight of God, he says, "Suku ngechele." He asks God to forgive him.

There is a phrase I have heard many times among the Africans which illustrates that they are aware of two forces — one for good and the other for evil. If a child is obedient to his mother, father and friends, the people will say that he is "omola wa Suku" — "a child of God." But if he is bad they will say he is "omola wonyoha" — "He is the son of a snake."

The natives are great believers in the immortality of the soul and even the little children are brought up to believe that there is a Supreme Being to be served with a greater reward after death. At certain times of the year feasts are held over the graves of the old people — especially of those that have been outstanding. The people dance and play for a week at the ceremonies, placing on the graves of those honored dead, food, cloth and some of their strong beer. These are signs of love which the spirits of the deceased come to observe and enjoy. They also believe to a degree in reincarnation — that the spirit of the deceased goes into a newly conceived child.

When an Ovimbundu is asked to define God, he will say: "Suku Unene. Eye fu, eye uqua henda." "'God is great. He is everlasting and is merciful."

Before Angola fell under the domination of Europeans, the natives had a high moral code. Stealing, murder and adultery were punishable by death because they were believed to bring a bad name to the whole tribe. Even today when such crimes are being judged by natives, the accused finds it very hard going. Even now, the children of a man who has been convicted of a crime will find it hard to get married. The native belief is that when a marriage takes place the entire families are joined, hence they are very strict about seeing that nothing evil comes into the family through marriage.

During the early days, it was as hard for a child born out of wedlock to get married as it was for a camel to go through the eye of a needle. He was not even allowed to cast his eyes at another's marriage ceremony. Such taboos served to keep the family straight and clean.

Even today you hear the old people of the tribes say that they are not going to allow their children to destroy their good names, and generally the father is held responsible for the acts and doings of his sons until they are about forty years old and have taken on the leadership of the village.

Once I asked an old man why the fathers were punished for what their sons do. He explained it was because the father had "brought the rascals into the world."

During slavery days, when a boy would not obey the teachings and rules of the family he was sold into slavery and shipped off beyond the seas.

It is really impressive what a high standard of disciplined morals the bush natives have been able to maintain through their taboos, charms and traditions.

For about ten years after we arrived in Galangue we never locked up anything, so honest were the natives.

Then, little by little, we discovered things were disappearing, so one day I complained to one of the villagers. "Mr. Coles," he informed me, "those are the Christians doing that." He was telling us that local codes of law and ethics were watertight in preventing even such petty abuses of law and order.

In America towns and villages are often started by dissatisfied people who pull out of their homes for reasons of persecution or dissension of some sort. So it is in Africa. Sometimes there is a young man who does not agree with the old chief. He may find a large group of young people who think as he does. They set out to establish a new village. They may go two or three hundred miles away among hostile people or a different tribe which they will have to fight. The men go ahead and do the fighting. The women and children remain behind until the new country has been conquered. Then houses are built and the women and children brought in.

There is one unique feature about the African village. The fire in it must always come from the mother village. This practice gives the people good luck and wards off dangers.

The man who leads the groups to their new homes is made village chief. The rest of the families are divided up into wards. In the average village there may be ten or more wards, with fifteen or so families to a ward. The heads of the wards along with some of the elderly men will act as advisors to the chief. Whenever there is an argument, it is studied and settled by this counsel. When the case is settled, the guilty party is called upon to pay a fine which may be an ox, pig or goat. Then he kills a pig. His adversary along with the chief and his counselors are invited in to sit at the same table and eat this "peace" hog. After that, the dispute is considered finished and is never to come up again.

Law and order is observed in the African village much more than is usual among the people of most countries because every bad act is considered to reflect not only on the man who committed it but on his family as well. Even though the father of a criminal or the man who is head of his ward will have to pay a fine, there is a moral stigma which may reach down into the whole life of the young man and his family. When it comes time to marry, a man who has been a thief has a hard time to find a bride because even if a woman wants him, she will think twice before running the risk of contaminating her whole family.

Choosing a wife is done in this way. A young man sees a girl he likes. He tells his father or his uncle that he would like to marry her. He may not have yet told the girl, but that is not necessary so long as the elders agree. If they agree, the bridal price is fixed. If the boy's family has cattle, goats, sheep and hogs, and the girl's parents belong in the upper class and feel that their daughter is a belle on whom they have had to spend a lot, the price may go as high as two oxen for the girl's father, and a blanket, five or six yards of cloth, two hoes and a gallon of palm oil for her mother. These things represent reimbursement for what the parents of the girl had to put out to get her to the place where she would be marriageable.

It is figured this way. The cloth, hoes and oil are the

things her mother used to bring her up from the time of birth to her marriageable status. She used up two hoes in feeding her, six yards of cloth in dressing her and the palm oil to keep her greased so she would be attractive. The oxen are judged to be roughly the father's share of the upkeep.

If the boy's parents are satisfied with the price, they will take half of the bridal price to the mother and father of the girl. This act seals the engagement.

Now the girl will go to live with an aunt, a married sister, or her grandparents. She will be given a field of her own to cultivate in sight of the field of one who is designated to watch over her. She is not even to go out for wood or water alone. Someone must be watching over her continually.

During this time of preparation, the girl makes up her kitchen and household ware. She weaves various sizes of baskets for carrying wood, corn and so forth and molds her pots for water, cooking and for table ware.

Before the couple marries, the girl is expected to spend two weeks or more with the boy's parents so they may find out to their satisfaction whether she is a good cook and an efficient field worker.

While the girl is undergoing this period of preparation, the boy friend is not sitting by idly. He builds them a new house and plows a large field so there will be plenty of food for his bride and him to eat.

On her wedding day, the bride is escorted to her new home by uncles, aunts and friends about two in the afternoon. For several hours the young man and girl sit and look at each other like two old alley cats. They don't speak a word and the door is left open for all to watch. The actual wedding ceremony consists of the couple eating a chicken together. After this they are considered man and wife.

Outside of the newlyweds' door is placed a small bowl with oil in it. Those who think the boy and girl are good and will be true to each other will come, dip their fingers in the bowl and leave a present. It may be money, a pig, goat or cow.

The food for the wedding feast, consisting of roast oxen, chickens and pigs, beans and pots of sweet beer, is furnished by the young man, along with the bride's wedding clothes. He may go in debt for three or four years, but that means nothing to him so long as the neighbors say that he fed them well.

After a couple has been married for a year and there is no sign of a little chicumbu or binda on the way, the parents of the boy will begin to say their son is throwing away his time and soon there is discord in the home. The Africans just do not face the fact that some people cannot have children.

In African daily life, the cards are stacked against the women. There is always an east opening or gate in the fence around the village which is low and narrow. Here the men leave and enter. The gate is too small for them to enter with large loads and too low for them to get in if they are carrying anything on their heads.

But on the west side of the village there is a gate for the women to go in and out. It is large, wide and tall, so they can enter with baskets on their heads. When they come home from the fields at eventide, their baskets may be filled with ears of corn, sweet potatoes, beans, pumpkin leaves. They may also be carrying loads of wood to cook the food with that evening. Many of the women have babies on their backs, in addition.

When the women get home and unload these burdens, they have to dash off again to the river with pots on their heads for water. No one would expect the husbands to carry water. Their gate is not high enough to get through with a pot on one's head!

While the women are running to and fro getting supper ready, the men are in the gathering room, shaping hoe handles for their wives or just talking.

The men do the hunting, build the houses and fences and clear the fields by burning about every three years. They do the smelting of iron and the forging to make hoes, axes, arrow heads and other necessities.

When the corn and beans are ripe, it is the men's job to take them to the trading centers. Since the first thing they usually buy is some cloth for their wives, it cannot be said they are entirely ungrateful for the women who keep them alive, but they really do treat them as chattels nine tenths of the time.

As the Christian Church pushes its way into the African villages, a changing attitude toward women is noted. There is a fairer division of labor. Less frequently does one hear the impatient male retort: "Am I not a man child?" The men begin to help the women by doing a share of the hard work in the fields. They sometimes bring wood, too, but

I have yet to see one with a pot of water on his head. Such work is considered ignominious.

There are some interesting village customs connected with death. To the African death is extremely meaningful because he sees in each passing a bereavement for the whole village, not for just one family. All the four to five hundred people in the village go into mourning for two days or more. At first the mourning bears resemblance to a festival of some sort, but when the body is finally taken to the grave, the whole village breaks down and weeps. Strangers passing by join in with the others, weeping and sobbing for an hour or more, then rising and going quietly on their way.

To the African, it is extremely important to be buried in his native village soil. Let two or three men be working away from home for several years. One dies. The others will cut off an ear or finger of the dead man and keep it until they return home. It is presented to the parents of the dead man and buried with the same ceremony as if the whole body were there.

Three or four days after a death all the deceased's friends and relatives descend on the bereaved family. Two hundred or more may come and spend at least two days. The grief-stricken family is compelled to feed them all the time they are there — a custom hardly conducive to bringing sunshine into the lives of the bereaved family!

When an Ovimbundu chief dies there is a special ceremony. Although the breath may have passed out of his body, a potentate is not considered dead until his head has been severed from his body. This is accomplished by hang-

ing the body from a joist in a room and leaving it there until the body drops, leaving the head tied to the beam. The
chief's skull is then taken down, cleaned and put into its
proper place in the line of skulls of former tribal kings.
Each village has a keeper of the skulls, which may number
30 or more. It is the duty of the keeper to know the history
of each chief and his entire family.

The remainder of the chief's body is interred in a special grave and when it has been properly laid to rest, huge
boulders are laid on top of the grave to keep wild animals
from digging it up at night.

After the passing of a great chief, there is always a special feast. The whole village and many others will come
to mourn. For a week, the people will eat, drink and dance.
Half a dozen oxen may be consumed in commemoration
of this great man.

Induction of the new chief means another week of drinking, dancing and drumming. The new chief must be a
member of the line of tribal kings. He is nominated and
chosen by the village elders.

All chiefs have four or five wives. They say that one or
two women just could not do the housework required for
a chief, with all his visitors. When he becomes a chief,
his wives help him find others. On the surface, the old and
new seem to get along all right, but deep down there is
always one woman toward whom the chief seems to lean.
The chief's wives usually work out a unique division of
labor so they are not all waiting on him at the same time.
During the hours that he is being waited on by wife No. 1
he cannot call on wife No. 2 or wife No. 3. In this way,

his home usually sets an example of peace for the whole village.

Each wife is expected to give the chief something from her corn and beans other than just food. One may give him a hat, another a shirt, another a coat, and so forth. When they have all contributed, he is quite dressed up.

The Ovimbundu people have practiced circumcision for many years. The boys are circumcised at the ages of five to eight. There is a special camp and time for this operation. It is done in the dry season when the weather is cold. There is a special man who performs the operation and he has a special knife that is very sharp.

The work is done at a given place so all the blood and foreskins of the little boys will be together. There is a loud thumping of drums during the ceremony to drown out the crying of the little boys, though some of them are brave enough not to cry and stand by watching all that goes on.

Each boy has a male nurse who after the operation takes two or three leaves from an umbula tree, resembling the red oak of North America. These he chews into a paste. Then he pastes up the penis of the child in the preparation, leaving a hole in the end large enough for the boy to urinate.

This paste is highly satisfactory in preventing bleeding and infection. Only a few of the dressings have to be changed and I have heard of only one death from infection and seen only three cases of serious infection. All of the little boys urinated at night and morning around the same tree. They did this until the tree died, then as a rule they broke up camp and went back to their villages.

During the time the boys are in camp, they sleep on the ground around open fires. When they are not sleeping they are singing, and learning the stories and history of their clan. In camp they do not wear a stitch of cloth.

Conducting this ceremony in a single place is symbolic in that it welds the boys together in a closer bond in the life of their tribe.

This homecoming celebration marks a turning point in the lives of little African boys. Now they are allowed to sit in the company of the men in the palaver house in the evening. They are not allowed yet to join in the big debates and arguments but they are now privileged to share equally with the men the feast and a little of the strong beer if they wish. Now they will get their first piece of new cloth.

Now, too, as the little boys grow, they can take part in the dances and songs of the Ovinganje. This organization in Angola is a secret society equivalent to that of the Mau Mau in East Africa. It is anti-women and anti-foreign. A woman is never allowed to stand and look at the men when one of the Ovinganje are dancing. They are expected to stay in their homes. If they should be going along a road and meet some of the men with their regalia on, the women are told they must run as though a lion were pursuing them. If they do not heed this warning, woe unto them that night. The Ovinganje will visit them that night and give them a sound beating.

If a man's wife seems to be becoming headstrong and getting too much rein sometimes, her husband will tell the Ovinganje and they will parade in full regalia some night around that man's house. When the women and children have gone to bed, they will enter the marked home and give the wife a good flogging. It may even be her own husband who beats her, but she will never know.

Because of its connection with the circumcision rite, the natives have great faith in the leaves of the umbula tree as a healing agent. They do seem to arrest blood and promote healing, though I found other African barks which applied to a cut stop bleeding more quickly than the leaves.

Still I must say that it appears to be a simple observation that if the natives knew something about general household sanitation along with their knowledge of the herbs of the bush, they would do a much more successful job of treating the sick.

The African has a system of smallpox vaccination that is simple and time-honored. When a case breaks out, the people of the village come to the victim. He opens a bump and takes a little pus from it and smears it into cuts on the arms of those who wish to be vaccinated. I have been told that as a rule the vaccination "takes."

In Angola there are several poisonous snakes but I have yet to see a man or woman who died of snakebite. When one is bitten by a snake he immediately puts a tourniquet between the bite and his heart. First he cuts the wound and sucks the blood from it. Then he sears the bite over with fire, and in order to protect his mouth against bad effects, takes some bark from an umbula tree, rich in tannic acid, and chews it. Next he takes some dirt from one of the anthills that abound in Angola and chews that. Finally, he washes his mouth out well and goes on his way, keeping the tourniquet on for a day or more, loosening it from time to time.

There are native skills in many fields in which the African is adept. For instance, the African has what seems to be an inherent ability to work iron and smelt it. The way they do it is this. First, they dig a trench about fifteen inches deep, and into it put charcoal to a depth of five or six inches. On top of the charcoal they place a layer of iron ore, perhaps two inches thick and then on top of that another layer of charcoal. The layers are repeated until the trench is full. Then it is sealed with a layer of earth and the whole thing packed down a little. Then holes are dug from the top of the trench to the bottom and tubes of fire clay run down into them. Bellows are used to blow down into these tubes. Each bellows has three or four men working on it but they work only one at a time. It may take two weeks to smelt this trench or iron ore. When it is done, the slab of iron is cut into as many pieces as there were blacksmiths working. They take it to their various shops and make it into hoes, axes, arrowheads, knives and needles.

The African has his own method of welding iron. First he places the end of the two pieces he is going to weld in a fire and heats them to a straw-brown color. Then he prepares a mud bath and puts the heated ends of the iron into it, keeping them there until they become black and cool. Then he puts the mud-encrusted ends into the fire and blows away until they reach a good welding heat. At this red hot heat the iron is taken out and beaten into shape.

What especially interested me was the use of the mud in welding. In modern industrialized countries, sand or a chemical is thrown into the fire on the iron when it reaches a certain temperature. This melts and forms a thin coat-

ing which keeps air from reaching the hot iron. If air hits
the iron while it is hot, a scale will form which will prevent
a good clean weld. The African's mud coating does the
same thing. The African method takes more time, but it
assures a good strong weld.

When an African blacksmith makes a knife for shaving
he works the iron while it is hot in powdered charcoal.
This gives carbon a chance to enter the molecules of the
iron while they are open and creates a high grade of carbon steel.

A tempering bath for the knife blade is prepared by
charring and beating into small pieces an ox's horn mixed
with the droppings from the henhouse. Then he adds
water and allows the mixture to stand overnight before
giving the blade a bath in it.

Who taught these Africans this simple but efficient
method of obtaining an ammonia bath from a charred ox's
horn? Who told them that chicken dung would furnish
the oil needed to close the molecules a little so the tempering process will not be too rapid?

As I learned the Umbundu language I tried to use it in
discussing things of nature with the people. One of our
favorite subjects was the birds and their habits. I cannot
give a list of all the names they gave me, but they knew
at least forty. They described the birds' songs, calls, nest-
ing habits, and showed me the food that each family group
ate.

Sometimes I thought the boys were "pulling my leg"
but I could always check their knowledge against someone else's. Those lads could put real birdlike feeling into
those calls, especially when it was the mating call. Some

said it was an "African instinct" but I think this ability came from long study and observation of birds in the bush.

In 1925 a Mr. and Mrs. Boulton were sent out to Angola by the Pittsburgh Museum to make a study and collection of birds, and in 1933 Harvard University sent one of its students to Angola to make a study of the gnawing animals of the colony. The natives with their wide knowledge of the things around them were a big help to these folks.

I thought one day I would see how many different rats Sekulu Chiwale could name. He was able to distinguish sixteen, giving their habits, food and other characteristics.

Among the Ovimbundu women as a rule are the potters. It is interesting to watch them prepare the clay and make a pot. They use a method that is basically the same as is used today in our schools of pottery and ceramics. When I saw the women of Angola grinding up pieces of old broken pots and working them into the clay for the bottoms of new pots, I thought this must be the result of some native superstition. But later when I returned home and studied pottery at Alfred University, I learned why they were doing it although they professed they did not know themselves. It was to prevent the clay from contracting so much that it would crack. Another lesson they have learned is to place the pots in the shade so they will dry slowly. If they are put in the sun they will dry too fast and crack. When the pot is dry, they rub it with cow's dung, then burn it. Usually they can't get high enough heat to make a glaze, but the dung helps a little.

When a native woman takes a piece of clay and rubs it through her fingers, then says it is good or not good — as if by instinct — you might as well take her word for it, I have found. The African woman's fingers just seem to know good clays.

Though the women use the same principles in making their pottery as are employed in other countries, their terms and words are absolutely different, which shows that the art is indigenous.

The women of the Ovimbundu tribe also make the dyes which are used in coloring their baskets, mats, cloth and rugs. The colors are fast and eye-catching. The dyes I have seen made have an iron oxide base but the color is vegetable. The different shades are brought out by different treatments.

To make a dark blue or black color, they use bog ore and boil it with a leaf they call *evava*. It looks like the ears of a dog. Each plant produces only two leaves, which lie flat along the ground.

I was very much impressed by the art of the Ovimbundu and their designs. Lines are straight and true and the native has an enviable eye for beautiful proportions.

I was constantly discovering new areas in which the Ovimbundu were much better informed, more talented, or more sophisticated than anyone who does not know the Africans could possibly imagine.

When I was doing medical work at Galangue I was truly amazed to discover how much they knew about the various parts of the body and their functions. Mrs. Jololo, about whom I have told earlier, was only one example of the natives who, without having received any European education at all, had what seemed to be an innate knowledge of anatomy and a real knack for medicine.

In the mission hospitals, African women are holding jobs as trained nurses, medical assistants and laboratory technicians, while native men have advanced to the stage in the medical profession where they administer anesthetics, take blood counts and perform other services at that level. At the Chilesso Hospital, under Dr. Mary F. Cushman, there was a native doctor and dentist, Dr. Sapunga, who even performed operations. Dr. Sapunga had received all his medical training from Dr. Cushman during the thirty years of splendid work she put in at Chilesso Hospital and had taken his dental training at Elat Mission in the Cameroons.

Because they start with a knowledge of anatomy in their native language, it is not difficult for the native boys and girls to grasp the science of medicine.

So too the African has a native background that stands him in good stead when modern education comes his way. I dare say an African never makes an error in grammar in his own complex language. If he does, it will very likely be said that he was born in a mission station.

Folklore and tales to stir the imagination are part of every African's village life. Every tribe had a special house in which the skulls of former rulers were kept and these were made the basis of the play life of the people. Every child can tell something of the history of his family and his tribe. Each evening there is a drama enacted, the girls playing by themselves and the boys by themselves. These stories concerning the lives of tribal kings or other great happenings of their history are full of dramatic situations and well worth seeing.

When it comes to music there is nothing more beautiful

than to hear an African woman singing a lullaby. She can reach anyone, soothing both the soul and the mind with her sweet melody.

Generally, the average native has some trouble with higher mathematics, but with effort he usually can make the grade.

Storytelling is one of the ways the natives have of fixing things in their minds and building a vocabulary. Then they play games with each other that serve this same purpose. For example, one man will say to his friend: "I ate oak for breakfast," and the other man will reply: "I had cow's meat for breakfast." So each time they meet and greet each other, the man who says he eats wood expects the other to match his wood with some different kind of meat. Thus they go through the lists of known animals and trees throughout their area.

There are some African habits of preserving food that are unique. For example, the native women know the art of making sweet potato meal. They cut the potato into thin slices and put them into a place to dry slowly. When they are thoroughly dehydrated the potato chips are placed in a bag made of leaves sewn together and hung in the kitchen where smoke can reach it. The smoke keeps the bugs out, as well as preserving the potatoes. The women dry and keep such things as pumpkin, beans, peas and cassava leaves by boiling them and squeezing them into balls to be placed in the sun to dry. These are put into bags and hung in the kitchen the same as the sweet potatoes. When these leaves are cooked their flavor and color are just about the same as when they were green.

The people gather mushrooms and dry them in large quantities each year. The children enter into this job because even a seven-or eight-year-old has been taught which are edible.

Since Africa is full of wild animals, one of the chief occupations of the menfolk is hunting. There are many brave men in this occupation, known as *ucongo*. The young man will follow an old hunter for two years or more, or until he has learned well the habits of the animals. Then he will go out for himself.

During the time of his apprenticeship he learns to walk upwind of the animal and not down. He learns to tell by the grass and weeds when an animal is running. During the dry season he learns to tell this from the way the leaves are thrown from the path of the animal. He can also tell if an animal is wounded by the way he walks.

Last of all the apprentice is introduced to the *etambo* — the temple of the fetish. This is a little house where some part of an animal is kept hanging more or less in the center of the building. Before an African hunter goes out he comes here to pray to the god of hunting. With all his knowledge of animals and their world, he hardly ever comes back home without his quarry.

Once while going through the bush about a mile from our mission I came across a perfect alfalfa plant. Was it native to the country or had some of my imported seeds been carried by the wind? I walked a little farther and came upon two or three more leguminous plants of a different type. Altogether I counted six or seven of these as I walked along to the Elombo River where one of my big farmers was preparing an old village site for beans. While I was talking to him, I noticed a bed of vines about twenty feet wide and forty feet long. Examining them I saw they belonged to the pea family.

This was in October — the peak of the dry season — in an area that had been burned off in July. Here were vines seven or eight yards long and under them was a leaf mold two inches thick.

I wanted to see the roots of these wonderful plants, so I got some men to help me dig them up. Some went five or six yards into the ground and were covered with nodules. Next day I took the plant eighty-five miles and had some pictures made of it. Its name, I found, was *Oka kunde kelunda*. I know it was a good smother crop and proved this by trying it out in my wife's rosebed where I nearly killed her roses within a year's time.

After discovering many of these rare leguminous plants, I decided to keep a record of them, with the help of one of the men in the village. We listed eighty-three different plants, each of some agricultural and pastural value.

The name of my native botany helper was Sekulu Kangombe ("little ox"). When he came to me, he was wearing two deerskins, but he certainly knew his plants. It was a great joy to me to learn from him. Not only was he a botanist but a zoologist of wide knowledge, too. It was interesting to hear him name the different insects, worms, butterflies and moths. No worm to him was a mere *ochipuka*; he knew what each kind was called.

The average traveler through Africa thinks he has seen a great deal if from a safari he views the wild life of the

country, hears the drums beat and sees the colorful native
dances. There are many things hidden just beneath the
surface that he does not see. In order to survive in Africa,
man has to learn to live in his environment, no matter what
may be in it with him. He has to work out means whereby
he can survive.

I saw much more, and I am convinced from my side-by-
side study with Africans that they are keen students of
their environment and highly cultivated in the lessons of
the world around them.

If the westerner is humble enough, he can be taught
much by the African about his world. He has a wide
knowledge of the things around him, and is not asking the
Christian to impose his western ways and civilization and
destroy his world. What he is interested in is learning the
Christian's economic, social and religious values. Of these
he will take what is right and discard the rest. He will
be able to judge what is right, I am convinced, only if we
meet him halfway to his world. We must show him the
beneficial results of our thinking right where he is.

7

Where Bread Grows on Trees

As Dr. Julian Rhea of the Methodist Mission in Portuguese East Africa told a conference in Madras, India, in 1938, "no man should be sent out to a mission who cannot load an oxcart with a pitchfork of manure."

This, I am convinced, is becoming truer every day as people awake out of the Dark Ages and demand better things. It is especially true in rural Africa where there are millions of head of oxen and only a handful of people who know how to train and drive them. The handling of oxen and plowing, in my estimation, should be a "must" for all missionary candidates who want to make themselves really indispensable to people who otherwise are ready to question the contribution of the foreigner in their midst.

I am not saying that any missionary should give up his Bible training to be an ox driver. These people need the word of God badly. They receive it eagerly. But at present they are thinking of a better life in terms of everyday things around them — food, clothing and better shelter. The missionary must see this and help them to meet these immediate demands.

This conviction of mine was confirmed during eighteen months my wife and I spent in Liberia in 1935-36.

Our stay there was the result of the Depression. Bad times at home forced the American Board to retrench by having the older missionaries come home and the younger ones transferred wherever they could best be used.

We in the Galangue mission received word in March that we were to leave in May. Bertha and I were loaned to the Booker T. Washington Agricultural and Industrial Institute at Kakata, Liberia.

This school, located on about one hundred acres of cleared land, fifty-six miles back in the hinterland from the Liberian capital of Monrovia, was just getting started when we were there. It had about forty students and most of them had hookworm, many had round worms and some had yaws. The morale of the place was very bad.

Dr. Anson Phelps Stokes, president of the Phelps-Stokes Fund in New York, while visiting in the South had met Mr. James L. Sibley, then serving as state agent for Negro schools in Alabama, and offered him the position of Supervisor of Education in Liberia to serve under all the American boards and societies working in Liberia which had set up an Advisory Committee on Education in Liberia.

One of Mr. Sibley's first jobs was to survey the educational needs of Liberia. Out of his study came plans for the founding of the Booker T. Washington Agricultural and Industrial Institute.

President D. B. King of Liberia proposed that the school be located at Kakata and that it be developed interdenominationally. At his request the Liberian Legislature granted one thousand acres of land. The Institute was incorporated in the State of New York on March 14, 1931, and the same year the Board of Trustees of the Booker T. Washington Agricultural and Industrial Institute was chartered by the Republic of Liberia. Support came chiefly from the Phelps-Stokes Fund and the Methodist Mission Board, though contributions have also been made by the General Education Board, the American and New York State Colonization Societies, and the Methodist, Lutheran, Protestant Episcopal and National Baptist Mission Boards. A number of substantial grants have also been made by the U.S. State Department.

At the Booker T. Washington Institute we found them trying to provide education and guidance closely related to the daily needs of the African people, just as we had been doing at Galangue. Courses were given in such practical subjects as agriculture and carpentry, in furniture making and bricklaying and mechanics. However, things weren't going along too well because many of the students and even some of the faculty doubted the value of such nonintellectual work.

Because of its limited budget, Booker Washington Institute has never had more than about two hundred students though thousands of African natives would like to study there and could certainly benefit their continent by so doing. Grades in the school run from the sixth through the twelfth.

Long after our time the Institute was transferred to the Liberian government at its request, to be incorporated as a unit of the University of Liberia.

We arrived in Liberia on May 3, 1935. How long we

had been looking for this little spot on the globe where Negroes had the first and last word! I remembered the time when I was a boy and the man from one of the Liberian colonization societies came to persuade my father to emigrate. He certainly didn't indicate we would have to work too hard. I recalled his description of Liberia as a place where "bread grew on trees." Naturally we thought he meant we would only have to sit under a tree and have bread fall in our laps. Later in Liberia I learned that he was referring then to the bread-fruit tree, which grows in the coastal regions, having been imported there from the Pacific. Altogether about thirteen thousand American Negro settlers did go out to Liberia, between 1820 and the Civil War, I believe.

We spent our first night in Liberia at the West Africa College where we were met with a great deluge of rain lasting an hour or more. The following afternoon we got a truck and set out for Kakata.

Today there is a good road to Kakata, but even now this village is considered an outpost of civilization. Beyond it are many small towns and villages made up of thirty to one hundred native huts, but they are only reachable by footpaths.

About half a mile from the school we had to get out of the truck and cross the Due River by means of a little native dugout. It was dark by that time and at one point my daughter Laura came within an inch of falling into the water, but we finally arrived.

After we had rested up, I met with the trustees of the Institute and told them my plans. I told them I needed some equipment including a brickmaking machine, tile press, sawmill and some woodworking machines. Right away the missionaries in charge said it wouldn't be possible. Other missionaries, they said, had brought such machinery out and it had rusted away on the docks.

I said: "That may be true, but the machinery I shall get will be at work six weeks after it reaches Liberia."

In fact, most of the people working at the Institute were discouraging. One white missionary who seemed to be in the good graces of the Liberians said to me: "Coles, there's just one thing I'd like to do at Booker T. Washington Institute. That's to go there and lock the place up and throw the key away."

At first there was some talk that I should be made head of the Institute but the Mission Board in New York wrote me the Liberians would object to having an American Negro at the head. I found out the source of the objection later and was glad to have it removed on the basis of the work I was able to do there.

When I was in Liberia, the American Negroes there were received by the natives not as brothers but as enemies. This was because at that time in Africa a man of another tribe was always regarded as an enemy. Moreover, many of the Americans had been guilty of exploiting the natives. The antagonism between the two classes created grave dangers and the Liberian government was trying to do something about it.

I fell right into the middle of that unfortunate situation, though I did meet some far-seeing people who were able to see above and beyond that problem, thank goodness. On

the way to Kakata, during a stopover at Accra on the Gold
Coast I had had several interesting talks with the paymaster
of the Police Force, about Africa in general. One day he
said to me: "Mr. Coles, the future of Africa is in the hands
of you American Negroes." I asked him to explain. "It's
like this," he said. "I am a Fanti and that man there is a
Shanti. Although we have been through school together
and we are both Christians, we cannot get together. You
have lost your tribal identity. You can care as much for
me as you do for this man. We will work with and around
you but we cannot do it if we are alone."

He went on to say he felt that God had sent some
Africans to America so we could learn the more advanced
ways of the white man and come back and teach them. He
wanted to know why more of us American Negroes had
not come back to teach the Africans.

Our first arrival in Liberia coincided with one of the
most interesting periods in that black republic's history.
It was the time of the League of Nations' investigation of
slavery in Liberia and that republic's heroic stand to remain
independent and free from big-power domination.

It all started when a book by Lady Kathleen Simon, wife
of Sir John, appeared in London in 1929, charging that
an organized slave trade existed in Liberia. The book,
Slavery, caused such a stir that demands were heard at the
League of Nations headquarters in general for immediate
replacement of the Negro government with a strong-
minded white one.

I myself have described the slavery I discovered during
my early days in Angola and I imagine that what existed

in Liberia in 1929 was somewhat akin to it. The chief of a native tribe can still command labor just as the Portuguese officials can from those unable to pay their taxes. I have described how tribesmen "pawned" out their children for an indefinite period when there was a period of famine. As far as they could see, this was the only alternative to letting the children die. Just when a native was working out his taxes and when his services had been forcibly diverted to private purposes was not always easy to detect.

Anyway, the United States government made known its horror at the reports of slavery in Liberia. President King vigorously denied them and appealed to the League of Nations for an investigation. A commission made up of the United States, Liberia and the League came under the chairmanship of Dr. Cuthbert Christy of the United Kingdom, went to Liberia, heard many imaginative and exotic tales from some 250 aborigines over a period of four months. It found "pawns" but no real slavery.

Liberian finances were at a low ebb at this point and the British proposed that the country be put into international receivership. They wanted the Liberian government to cease to function. The Liberians said flatly there should be no assistance that would end their political independence.

Soon after my arrival I visited the President, Edwin Barclay, who had succeeded President King when he resigned after the 1930 League report on Liberian slavery.

President Barclay was a fine upstanding man. Right away he said: "Mr. Coles, I know what is on your mind so I shall tell you the whole story of our relations with the League of Nations. We asked the League for a loan but we got a plan of assistance that would have ended our political independence. Before I turn Liberia over to the League of Nations," he declared, "I will suffer my head to be cut off. If they come to take it by force, I will not resist, but to sign it away, that I shall never do."

I have met many men, and for many have had great and deep respect. Yet my feeling for this little short man of color went deeper than just ordinary respect or honor. I had something of the same feeling the free world had when during World War II we heard Churchill say, "We shall go on to the end . . . We shall fight . . . on the beaches, we shall fight on the landing-grounds, we shall fight in the fields and in the streets . . . We shall never surrender . . . "

Standing there in the presence of President Barclay of Liberia, I know that here was a man who had not wronged any of his fellow beings but was going to stand by his moral guns and shoot in defense until the barrel dropped off.

It turned out in the end that the answer was Harvey Firestone. By direct negotiation between Firestone and Liberia the problem was finally solved. Firestone had come out to Liberia in 1926 after the British had forced up the price of rubber he needed for his automobile tires. The British-Dutch rubber monopoly was a hard nut to crack but great American business geniuses — Firestone, Thomas A. Edison, and Henry Ford — wouldn't be beaten. They all had their ideas for getting around that monopoly. Firestone negotiated with the Liberian government for 1,000,000 acres of land at six cents an acre that would be his for ninety-nine years. He would pay an export duty to the Liberian government on each ton of rubber exported. This income had not really gotten under way when the government started, which is the reason it had its financial difficulties.

After the Firestone-Liberian agreement was renegotiated and a loan made to the government, Liberian revenues improved immediately and so by 1934 the government was making regular payments on its indebtedness, the rubber plantations were expanding and thousands of employees were being taken on to tap rubber trees. Liberia's sovereignty was intact.

After a month in Liberia, we returned to Boston and New York to consult the local trustees of the school to see just what was expected of us and what we could get in the way of equipment.

I asked to be allowed to take out to Kakata the following: an ox wagon, a set of blacksmith tools, blower and anvil, a portable sawmill, a tractor, a brick and tile machine and a power pump. Also I asked to be allowed to put up a tank with a capacity of at least 25,000 gallons of water.

The trustees of the Institute said they would recommend this list of equipment but they expressed grave doubt of the place of such simple farm tools in the life and work of the Institute. My thoughts went back to those people over in Africa who had also insisted that such equipment would rust away on the beaches in Monrovia.

"The machinery I shall get will be at work six weeks after it reaches Liberia," I said in a quiet voice.

I also wanted to take in sixty more pupils to add to the

forty in the Institute and I wanted to take them in at the first-grade level but no one could see how this could be done without increasing the teaching staff, and for this there was no money.

The boys they were taking in were boys who had been living with people who knew the value of an education, since they had already been through several years of school. I wanted to take in the boys from the bush who knew nothing about school.

At that time there were classes only for half a day. The boys worked the other half. I recalled the long hours of combined work and study I put in at Snow Hill and Talladega and suggested a plan. I would start a night school. The older boys would not work in the mornings any more but would teach in the night school, using the mornings to prepare the lessons. The night school pupils I would use during the day to get out material for the large building program and to develop the farms. This way more boys could go to school and I guaranteed we would save money in both the development of the farm and the assembling of building material. The Institute's Board of Trustees saw the wisdom in this and let me go ahead, but Mr. Firestone and Owen D. Young who were members of the board told me: "Mr. Coles, if you do only half of what you have told us, we will be satisfied."

I got my equipment too, including the portable sawmill and tractor which Mr. Firestone himself gave.

Dr. Thomas Jesse Jones, educational director of the Phelps-Stokes Fund and Mr. L. A. Roy, Dr. Jones's assistant, gave me advice on the clothes I should take out to

Liberia. One item they recommended was a full-dress suit. They said I would need that for "state occasions." I acquired one, but praise God, I have never had it on since the night the tailor fitted it on me. Africa just isn't the place for dress suits. Dungarees are much more suitable for the job that needs to be done there.

I arrived back in Monrovia on January 9, 1936.

After two days in Monrovia I left for Kakata with a truckload of equipment which I had brought out with me. At that time the roads were rough and the bridges were not to be trusted over small streams but we arrived safely with our new treasures.

As I began to unload the machinery, I could see the people's eyes opening. They had never seen such machinery at a school before. They seemed to feel that it would open a new world to them.

One morning in February 1936, Dr. Claude A. Reupel, who was principal of Booker T. Washington Institute at the time, received a radiogram saying the budget for the year had been approved and we could begin working on our program. Dr. Reupel was principal of the school, director of education and building. My wife and the late Mr. George S. Best were his assistants in the school work. Mr. William A. Corbin was in charge of building construction. I had charge of the agricultural work and extension program and the tile and brick yard. Mr. Best was my assistant with the farm work.

When we received the good news that the budget was assured I worked out my program for the development of the farm and agricultural extension work. We were going to expand the cotton field to five acres, peanuts to four acres, sugar cane to ten acres, cassava to ten, rice to five, and the garden to three acres. Also there was to be a large coffee, banana and palm oil nursery, with an eye to eventually furnishing the country people with a standard variety of plants. We were also going to carry on some experimental work in cotton and peanuts.

But soon after tailoring our plans to a $16,000 budget we received word that the money would not be available. What a letdown! On the heels, however, followed another cablegram stating that Mr. Firestone had said that if the Phelps-Stokes Fund and others would raise $5000, he would give the rest. There was rejoicing again as we "set our sails for the other side."

Right away I began to assemble my new night school students. I had decided to take in sixty. The first job was to get classroom space for them. The cottage of the director of the school was built high up off the ground, in African style. So after a little digging, we were able to put in a cement floor. We installed several good steel windows which had been left over from the building of the cottage. Soon we had four large airy classrooms which cost only the labor plus a few dollars for cement. The students did all the unskilled work.

My night school students were my pride and joy. Because it was cooler at night, they seemed to be able to apply themselves better than the other boys. Then too, they knew they had to make good so they would not let me down. I was happy about their co-operation because my night school idea was on trial.

Thanks to their ability and diligence, many of the boys in a year and a half had been put in the fourth grade. Those boys did not fail me. They had to earn their board and keep in addition to their studies. We started them on assembling stones for the foundations of two buildings, cutting lumber, making brick and tiles for the buildings and on the opening up of the farm we put out ten acres of cassava — a staple of the Liberian diet — four of rice, two or three of cotton, three of sugar cane and three of corn.

Our sugar cane and corn were planted in the lowland on the Due River, land which had not been used because of the heavy brush and superstition. We went in and cut the trees and underbrush and got the wood out and used it to bake our tiles and brick. Then we set fire to the brush and burned it off as the natives do.

One day, talking to Mr. Corbin, one of the teachers, I mentioned that we needed a stump puller to help clear the land. He said that he could make something to fill the job. In ten days time he had a machine ready. Mr. Corbin had once had a course in Boston in boatbuilding so he drew on his knowledge of the principle involved in pulling ships into drydock. The equipment he was able to rig together we used not only for clearing the land but for pulling clay up the hill to be made into tiles and brick.

Mr. Roy was visiting the Institute at the time and before he went back to New York I told him I would like to have 600 or 700 feet of steel cable for the school. In New York he called up one of the large hotels and got a thousand feet of discarded cable quite reasonably.

After that, when it came time to yank stumps, we put the capstan in place, then ran the cable out 300 to 400 feet and made half-hitches on three or four small stumps at a time. Six men would heave away on the lever and up would come the stumps. We cut the guy roots of larger stumps so we were able to get out trunks of trees as large as twenty-four inches in diameter. All these we burned to make our bricks and tiles.

In a few places in this bottom land, we had to put in both open and blind ditches to drain the fields. Those who saw them thought we had accomplished a great feat in "agricultural engineering" though it was a comparatively simple operation.

To get the logs to the tile yard, I rigged up the logging wagon which I had brought out from New York and forged yokes and chains for five yokes of oxen. Some of these had been trained, so I had to train only four or five. Both the natives and Mr. Roy were intrigued at the sight of three or four large logs being loaded on a wagon and carried away up a hill to the tile yard to be sawed into lumber.

Why should this be such a remarkable sight in Africa? It almost breaks my heart to see men having to hoist large logs on their shoulders and struggle with them hundreds of yards when out there in the fields there are ten or twelve big strong oxen walking around grazing. That is why I say the handling of oxen and plowing should be a "must" for all missionaries.

Our cotton crop ripened during the middle of the dry season, but we did not gather it. We wanted the people to see it. It was as good as any to be found in the southern states. We planted Stone Mountain #2 seeds. They did very well indeed. There was no rust on it nor any other type of disease.

Just because of this one display of cotton, the Board of Trade of Monrovia asked me to write the American Board and ask if we could come back just to demonstrate to the people how to grow cotton. Mr. J. H. Jackson, of Careysburgh, Liberia, especially wanted to learn because he intended to put in a gin and later looms to make cloth.

Seeing the zeal of the people over the growing of cotton I tried to interest them in peanuts and bananas — something that wouldn't have to be processed. I went to Monrovia and talked with some of the business heads. The director of the French House there said his company would buy every peanut the country could grow at $3 to $4 per hundredweight. He said he would buy every pound of bananas Liberia could produce also. At the time Liberia's national debt was $2,500,000. I started a slogan like this: "Grow a million bags of peanuts and pay off your national debt." I went from town to town preaching this on Sundays. I also spread the message to every man I met on the road.

It was not long before almost every man I met would invite me to come down to see his "peanut farm." True, some of them were no larger than a blanket, but they all showed signs of effort.

The African people only need someone to lead them and give advice. I found them to be very good workmen but they needed a leader, an objective. Firestone's work is proof of this.

The Firestone plantation in Liberia today is doing more than just getting rubber out of the country. The young men are being taught trades which will stand them well wherever they may go. Among the Liberians in Mr. Firestone's employ today are first-class brick masons, carpenters, automobile drivers, mechanics, nursery men, trained nurses, bookkeepers, and trained store workers.

When the Republic of Liberia set itself to the task of raising the standard of education of its people a few years back, Firestone Plantation was among the first to embrace the program. It is also doing notable work in the field of health and religion.

Mr. Firestone took the lead in Liberian rubber production but today there are individual Liberian rubber growers who are making $100,000 a year on their rubber. And what is being done with rubber could, I say, be done by the people in the development of peanuts, cotton, sugar cane and bananas. These are salable farm commodities in the production of which whole families can take part without any capital outlay.

One day a radiogram arrived from New York saying a 25,000-gallon steel water tank was on its way for the school. Mr. Firestone cabled us that if we would put in the foundation, he would have his builder put up the tank. So Mr. Roy got busy and within ten days we were pouring the concrete for the foundation. A few days later Firestone engineers came to assemble the parts of the tank. For a month the air hammers sang there in Kakata.

Until today, the most imposing landmark to be seen in the interior of Liberia from Monrovia to the French border is the water tower of the Booker T. Washington Institute. It has become a beacon light to those who ventured into the hinterland. Three weeks after the men had driven the last rivet, pipes had been laid and fresh sparkling water was finding its way into the dormitories and homes of the teachers. It truly marked a new day in the lives of these young Africans.

About five months after Mr. Roy and I had started our work at the Institute, two missionary ladies from one of the boards working in Liberia visited us. While they were there from out of the blue they made this confession: "We were the ones who sent that cable to the Board in New York stating that the Liberian people did not want an American Negro at the head of the Institute. We were sure Mr. Coles would be either with the government and against us or with us and against the government. Either way we feared there would be trouble. But we see now that he is all right. He is just a 'Christ workman.' "

As I look back now, I can see my program seemed drastic to some people who thought missionaries should only preach, and frightened them. But I am convinced that Christian missionaries must not be afraid of progress and giving people what they need. Certainly God would not want it that way. The Liberian people themselves had no objections. They were willing to follow me, no matter where the path might lead. Many a time while I was there men and women both would say to me: "Professor Coles, I want to send my boy to Booker Washington Institute." My reply was: "We will be glad to have him but remember he will have to work because we all work at B.W.I."

They were always anxious to have their boys become "engineers." That was a high-sounding word they had learned from the Firestone men.

As we worked, the Institute took on new life and color. People from the surrounding country liked to come and visit us. Some of those missonaries who had said that the school should be closed told me they now wished they had accepted the principalship.

The deepest impression on the Liberian people as a whole was made when the industrial department of the Institute put on an exhibit at the inauguration of President Barclay in July 1936. When the President heard we were making roofing and flooring tiles at B.W.I. he had said he wanted to be the "first man to stand on the flooring tiles made in Liberia." So we built a little platform for him to stand on when he was taking the oath of office. It was a dramatic and historic occasion. It was historic because these were the first flooring tiles made in the country. It was dramatic because here was a man who had saved Liberia from the big powers and preserved its independence during those days of great agony.

We built a small brick house and covered it with roofing tiles of Liberian clay made at the Institute.

A lot of people were skeptical when I first talked of making tiles at the school. One of the men thought they would not hold up in Liberia. I told him about those we made in Angola where the rains were just about as heavy as in Liberia. He remembered an old French Legation building covered with tiles and suggested we go look it over. Although it had been deserted for some time the tiles were as good as new. They had been on the building forty years or more. Of course they were made in France, but I assured this gentleman ours would be just as good. So I was allowed to get the tile press.

We had other things in the exhibit for the President, among them a plow, with parts, hoes, and axe and chopping knives. When the people saw these things they said their boys just must attend the Institute, even if they had to work hard.

One hot sunny morning, we received a radiogram stating that we had to return to Angola. Our pupils at the Institute expressed their sadness and we tried to work out means whereby we could stay for the three years that had been contracted for, but Mrs. McDowell, in Galangue, was ill and the American Board said we must return.

Eighteen months is a very short time to try to judge a people and their cultural trends, but I was able to observe a few facts both about the Americo-Liberians and the native Africans. The wall between these people is in fact breaking down and a social, educational and economic unity is being evolved. Today the native Liberian is to be found in all departments of the government, in the schoolroom and in the professions.

Many Americo-Liberians have adopted native youngsters who enjoy the same privileges as the other children in the family. The adopted child takes the name of the family and is sent to school just as the other children are. There are even cases where these native-born children have been sent to Europe or America to be educated. Conversely, the Americans have adopted native patterns of art, music and dancing. Intermarrying is becoming the order of the day between the two groups. I have even heard of cases where Americo-Liberians belonged to some of the native secret orders.

At the rubber plantation there were young men and women from mission schools who had gone on to get degrees from colleges in both Europe and America in law, education, theology, civil and mining engineering, but when I looked into their homes I did not find even a pin which was made in Liberia by the Liberians. That fact worried me. The sugar they used daily came from Europe or America. Their salt is imported, yet the same ocean from which it was made washes the shores of Liberia. The dishes on their tables are imported but the country has good clays for making tableware. Their shoes are from Europe or the United States, yet their swamps are full of mangrove trees, rich in tannic acid with which their own leather could be tanned.

I was told in Liberia that in the early days that country had a favorable balance of trade with the United States because of the brown sugar it shipped in big quantities. Then they made their own brick and other everyday articles, but today everything is imported.

For this I believe the blame must go partly to the Christian missions. The missions have proved that the Africans are able to grasp higher learning in the fields of the sciences, theology and law, but they have failed to teach the people how to meet their everyday needs. As a result, the Church in the underdeveloped areas of the world is daily losing ground to other agencies.

One thing I learned in Liberia was that I, an industrial and agricultural missionary, or as we call it today a "Point IV man," was playing a pioneer role that most of the other missionaries didn't understand.

A League of Nations report on Liberia had said: "Liberia's future depends on the prosperity of the small native cultivations. If model villages were erected near the plantations, cultivable land allotted and seed and machinery advanced, if these villages were furnished with the conveniences and amenities of a normal and healthy family life, there is no doubt that natives would leave their miserable forest homes and become regular plantation workers." They predicted too that "the educated native child will not try then, as he does now, to escape from his debased environment and loaf about the coast looking for a job in government offices already overcrowded with Americo-Liberians." This was practically the same thing I had been saying about the unfortunate flow of our rural people of Angola to the big cities of South Africa.

I left Liberia convinced that toil with the hands in behalf of one's brother man must buttress church work. It's no good preaching too long to one who is hungry. In Liberia, when the businessmen of Monrovia wanted me to stay to experiment with cotton-growing among the natives, I could have turned my back on the Church but that was not my desire. I was just a Christian man who loved to preach but also to work with my hands.

I am convinced from my many years of experience in Africa that only a changed missions program will meet the problem. Only as we teach the people of these countries the things that we know will help them to practical achievement of their everyday needs will we have any chance of leading these people to follow us in the Christian way of life.

Today jet planes have brought Africans and Americans within hours of one another. Foreign students from that continent are finding their way into our homes and colleges. New agencies have sprung up to tell the people what we missionaries used to tell them they either were not ready for or did not need. Young people are beginning to ask: "If it is good enough for you, why cannot we have it too?" My African friends have shown their capacity to use many things they do not yet have.

On my arrival in Monrovia, I saw ships unloading pots and other small cast-iron items marked "Made in Holland." Yet I knew that Liberia had high grade iron ores in several parts of the country. It was then I got my ideas about the necessity for introducing iron smelting at Galangue, a determination I was finally able to do something about when the war came and I went back to the United States.

8

Scrub-Up Week

A HIGHLIGHT of the year for the natives in Angola is "scrub-up" or "village improvement" week. This is the time when the local Portuguese officials or chefes come around and write up the tax rolls, and take a local census. You can imagine all the fuss and bustle that goes on getting ready for them!

The "hut tax" in our area of Portuguese West Africa was usually 80 to 100 angolares or $4 to $5. All men of sixteen or over had to pay. This was equivalent to about four months plantation work for the average native, or about one third of his annual income. This is a heavy burden and naturally there is considerable anxiety and fear, mingled with the challenge of putting the family's best foot forward for the gala day.

Big preparations are made. Native huts are given a new coat of gleaming white clay. Pigs that usually run through the streets are shut up in their pens. Crews of men go out and fill up the mosquito-breeding holes along the roads and a triumphal arch of palm is erected at the village entrance.

The entire male population of the village escorts the chefe to the desk in his special house for the "writing up" of the taxes. The old tribal chief is dressed up for the occasion. He has five or six yards of print cloth draped around his waist and reaching to the ground. Over that he wears a long shirt with the tail hanging outside down to his knees. Completing his costume he will have a coat and hat with a bright-colored feather on it. On his feet he wears a pair of sandals of a pattern dating back to biblical days. The young men usually wear a pair of nondescript trousers and a shirt and hat, if one is to be found.

The women fix themselves and their children up for the occasion. The women and older girls pour palm oil on their hair to give it a glistening effect. They call it *ulamba*, or glory. Some of it runs down on their bodies where it is rubbed in to chase out the dirt and make the skin look smooth. Sometimes the cleanliness extends only in a circle around a face, but at least they have all made some effort to show their respect for their visitor.

Some of the ladies wear dresses that may have come from New York or Lisbon. The fact that these may be two or three sizes too large bothers them little. Yet there are definite signs that women are women, even in the jungles of Africa. I have seen women with scraggly locks take combings from a woman with a fine head of hair and fasten them to their own hair to make it look more beautiful.

Festivities connected with the chefe's visit go on for a

week or ten days. There will be lots more meat than the average African sees at any other time because in Africa healthy animals are rarely killed for food. There will be roast pork, lamb and beef and if the men of the tribe have had any luck at hunting there will be some kind of wild meat. There will be beans and corn meal mush, and sometimes sweet potatoes. And to wash all this down there will be strong beer and sweet beer.

Strong beer is made from fermented corn, and despite the large amount consumed there is hardly ever a fight or other unbecoming behavior. If anything untoward happens it can almost always be traced to a native who has drifted back from the cities where he has been living with the Europeans.

As soon as the chefe has gone, the people say to each other: "Quenda olonoma vi kasi loku tu kevalela ño, u oku vi sika" — "The drums are ready and are only waiting for someone to beat them." Then they call in the people from two or three neighboring villages and the dancing and merrymaking begins.

As soon as the gaiety had begun to subside, I would appear on the scene. Some of them may have looked upon me as an austere "voice of conscience," but I knew this was the time to remind the men that as soon as they had paid this year's tax, they should begin looking for their tax money for next year.

I used to tell them that the Portuguese official was like a lion. "When you hear a lion," I would remind them, "you always move on ahead. You don't wait for him to catch you, then try to run. Once he has got hold of you it is too late. So it is with the tax collector," I said. "It will be too late to start getting the money together when the official comes."

After about two years of such talk around Galangue, I got the idea over. I am proud to say that now when the local official writes up the taxes in our area, ninety-five per cent or more of the men have the money in their hands, or waiting in boxes in their homes. There has been quite a change. Not only do the men have the tax money but some of them actually take the tax-collecting ritual in their stride. They are more interested in using the money that is left over to buy cattle and send their sons to school in faraway places.

One man who was not much worried about taxes was Senhor Silva de Sachipembe. One day in 1933 when he was recuperating from an operation, sitting under a tree, I got to talking to him. He had bought some peanuts. I saw him with them. I asked him what he was going to do with them. He said he was going to take them to Nova Lisboa, parch and sell them.

"Don't do that," I said. "Plant them instead. When they are ripe you can gather them, and then parch and sell them. Then you will have enough money to buy an ox-cart and oxen and haul wood and charcoal and sell it to the people of Nova Lisboa."

I didn't think he would do it, but that little spark caught fire. The following year Senhor Sachipembe showed up at my home. "You know what you told me to do with the peanuts?" he asked. "Well, I did it. I have bought an oxcart and am now on my way to the Ganguela country to get some oxen."

I thought up one scheme that helped a great many of

the natives. I told them to get a pig and name it Elesimu. That is Umbundu for tax money. Then I told them they should set out a field of sweet potatoes for Elesimu and not let a soul get a sweet potato out of it so long as Elesimu was alive. Some people think African pigs are a nuisance since they get underfoot and come into the houses, but at tax time they are a mighty good thing to have. Besides many of them do not get enough to eat and are runts. I told the people they were not to kill Elesimu until he was two years old.

Some people think the Portuguese system of taxes has been unnecessarily hard on the Angola natives but there are two sides to that question. In some ways, certainly, the system has been the making of the natives. It has made the men get out and work. Before these people were required to pay the "hut tax" they never had enough to eat, and they all went practically naked. Now, once a man has earned enough for his taxes, he almost always has enough corn and beans left over to eat or to sell and get himself some clothes.

Once I saw a chefe set fire to a man's clothing. On the surface this action seemed quite cruel, but the man's outfit was made of bark cloth which is an old-fashioned way of doing things, even in Angola. This cloth is made by taking the bark of trees, soaking it and beating it until it is soft and pliable. I myself encouraged the use of bark cloth among the natives because I figured if they wore that they could save money until they could get ahead in other more necessary fields. For instance, I thought they needed blankets before they needed woven clothing. But that chefe wanted to see the native put himself into textiles right away. That is why he took such drastic action. Sure enough, the next year, when the chefe arrived, the man was wearing regular clothes.

When the tax collector comes to the village he enrolls all the boys who have just turned sixteen so he can collect from them the next year. I have seen line-ups on tax paying that were a mighty funny sight, with sixteen-year-old girls but no men except the old fellows. If the chefe asks where the boys are, the natives just say there aren't any. They don't seem to realize that they are only exasperating the Portuguese official and preparing future trouble for the men who have paid their taxes.

While I never took sides either with the Portuguese or the natives in this difficult system, I always told my people that they might as well learn to "play the game." I would tell them that back in America everyone recognized that they had certain civic responsibilities. For instance, I said, if there was a dead dog on my property, I couldn't just let it lie there. It was my duty to remove it. I told them that it is their civic responsibility to help the Portuguese develop roads in their area, and the smartest Portuguese chefe I ever saw was one who divided his road work into sections and explained to the natives who were forced to work on it: "That's your section. You're responsible for that." They understood, and have built there the best stretch of road in all Angola today. Contract labor, I feel, will gradually disappear when the natives have shown they they have the ambition and the industriousness to stand on their own feet economically. Then they will have their tax money ready each year and no one will need to go off to work on the big European plantations.

The Portuguese government defends its action in compelling the Africans to work instead of sitting "blowing into the fire" or watching their wives till the tribal lands. They argue that it is a civilizing process since it gives responsibilities.

As it is, there is considerably more freedom in the contract labor system than the outside observer might suspect. Often I advised young men to report to the county seat for such work before they were called up. I would explain to them that they would get something like 40 angolares or $1.30 a month "throw away" money. I would tell them to save that. They not only would work off their back tax money but would come back to the village with tax credit for the next year. They could bring back in addition a couple of pieces of cloth and they would be freed from their tax nightmares so they could begin to save toward a bicycle or a plow.

Believe me, when I get among the natives I am a benevolent despot. I preach to them in the morning but in the evening I am cursing them out. One of the worst things you can do to an African native is to curse him out before women.

In the African language there is no such thing as a word for a lazy man. Not that they aren't lazy but they just don't like to be reminded of it. They talk instead about a man "who blows in the fire." I wait until I get them before women, then I call them an *o-chi-shin*. That is a strong word. Pretty soon, they are saying, "Tell us what to do. We're ready to do it."

Once you get the people's confidence, they'll do anything you tell them to. I guess I have been able to do this
because these everyday Africans have examined my philosophy and found it to be sound. They know that I
won't tell them to do anything that is not for their own
good.

So when I tell them to go to the Portuguese and put
their names down for contract labor, they go because they
know that then they are on the way toward getting plows
and oxen.

One Portuguese I heard about had five hundred men
working for him from four counties. He had in his safe
a little over 1000 contos, or something over $30,000. If that
money were properly reinvested back into the Angola
country, we could really begin to go places.

Sometimes the women are sent out to work on the roads
by the tribal chief. That shocks outsiders. It may merely
mean the men are all off hunting. I have made a road-
ditching plow and a grading scoop that can do four to
five miles of ditching in one day. You can see how much
back-bending labor such a machine saves. If I could make
enough road equipment, neither the men nor the women
would have to work on the road.

When a man is sent to work on contract labor, the
money he earns is sent back directly to the local official at
his county seat so it will be there when he needs to pay
his taxes. The record of the time he has put in is called his
tabella. After his back taxes and his tax for next year have
been deducted, the worker gets the rest of the money.

I can think of a lot of things that are wrong with this
system but there are also some good sides to it. Certainly

some are sent into contract labor who ought not to be sent. A man may have a plow and a bicycle and be getting up in the world and be sent by his native chief. When the Portuguese find out that he has made that much progress they are apt to send him back to his village. Also, there should be places provided for families to accompany workers and there should be schools for the children. That would encourage many men to go and lend weight to the Portuguese insistence that the real purpose of the system is to teach men to work. I am certain that they have a good object in view but there is too much leeway left for exploitation.

I have tried to instill into my friends in Africa a feeling of building up their lives as they would a house. I tell them they may have to suffer some while the foundations are being laid but in the end they will find they have made something beautiful. Back in America, I say, we Negroes in the South had to give ten free days to roadmaking back at the turn of the century. I myself did that in Alabama. I tell them it would be impossible for the Portuguese officials to chase all around to see if some local boss is being officious. One mulatto Portuguese I knew did just that and when he found a local boss violating his order of "no women on roadwork" he beat him. After that he introduced wheelbarrows on that road, and boy, was it a good one! It was the best in that whole section.

I am convinced, as are many people, that the emancipation of women is an integral and necessary step in the liberation of Africa. The fact that women plow the fields and do so much of the heavy work comes about from the pre-

occupation of men in the fighting of wars, hunting, and
making tribal laws. But now the African men's duties have
diminished in their onerousness. The tradition of women
doing all the land work is an anomaly in today's society.

My main accomplishment I think has been to teach these
people something about the dignity of labor. Some of this
has meant cutting through old taboos and superstitions
but where there is good to be gained from these we have
encouraged the people to keep the good and discard the
cannibalism and barbaric features. My work in Africa
began at a time when the native was ready to emerge from
his old superstitions and taboos. The old fellows talk freely
with me and as a result I have a pretty good picture in my
mind of primitive conditions as they were not more than
a generation or two before I arrived on the scene.

Some of these local customs aren't too bad. Though
they involve superstition and fear, sometimes they are
based on principles that make for the people's progress.

For instance, an African today who wants to become
a great farmer or hunter will seek out a man who has the
"charm." He finds him through the guild system. Each
guild has its "medicine" or fetish.

A man who has the "charm" and hence lots of food,
cloth and cattle, is known in his area as *Nasungila* (I lead).
Nasungila is a wise man. First of all, he knows that hard
work pays good dividends.

I have seen some of these men, these Nasungila, and I
would not disturb their system for anything because it
produces such good results.

The student goes and lives with his teacher for a year,

agreeing that he will carry out to the letter all instructions. During this time, the sun never finds the student in bed. He is in the field by the time the sun is up, and he works until about five in the afternoon. Nasungila tells him that if he doesn't work, the spirits will descend on him and kill him. Before long he has a feeling for real work in his bones.

Before the trainee graduates he is given a little bag full of dust, supposedly made from the powdered flesh of a baby. The story goes that Nasungila has robbed the grave of a baby, dried the flesh and ground it to powder.

Each understudy gets a little bag of this powder. Just before planting time, he puts a little of the dust in the palm of his hand and goes out at night to blow a little of it to the four corners of each one of his fields, to make them fertile. After that he begins his hard work, convinced that if he is lazy on the job, the spirit of that dead baby will descend on his head and cause his death.

After a year's training in the art of hard work, he too becomes a Nasungila, still bound by fear to the spirit of those dead babies, but an advocate of the theory that I have always preached, that "labor, whether of the head or the hand, is divine."

Under the same kind of system, the young men will follow the old hunter for two years or more, learning the habits of the animals. It is because of local customs and taboos such as these that I feel it is wrong to impose work habits from above. The Africans need to be taken by the hand and led. Habits of thought cannot be changed overnight and why, indeed, in cases where they produce such good results and do no harm, as with the Nasungila, should they be?

Many times the natives at Galangue have talked with me about how the white man treats them. When they complain of their Portuguese masters, I say: "Yes, they got into Angola because when you fought them you had only bows and arrows. They had guns and powder. Naturally they overcame you, but you still have in your hands three of the most powerful weapons with which to fight for equality, brotherhood and freedom that I know of. You have the word of God, the opportunity for education and you have work. Get them at any cost and you will be able to measure up to any man." I don't consider that such advice is seditious.

I have given much thought to the question of colonial governments in Africa, certainly one of the big problems of our times. As I look back over the centuries I say to myself, "Suppose the governments had not broken up tribal wars and subdued the natives?" Today, instead of a people clamoring for independence and recognition, they would still be as they were 1000 years ago, cursed with continual warfare, witchcraft and tribal autocracy.

If the white man has done nothing more in Africa than break up tribal wars, it has been worth his being there. A man named Chiwaili Melenga has told me something about how it was when he was a boy. When his family went to bed at night, they never knew whether they would wake up or be burned to death in the night. The enemy used to come in the night and throw fire on the thatched roofs and if the family ran out they would be met by warriors standing there with bows and arrows ready to shoot them.

Yet there needs to be an awakening on the part of both the African and his colonial masters. The natives need to give credit to the colonial governments where it is due. They must recognize that the white man has brought them roads, education, medical service and a common language.

At the same time, the colonial governments must recognize that the African natives are not babes. They have got to be treated as men and women and to be conscious that the time will inevitably come when they will want to help govern themselves.

9

Assimilados

In 1920 when the Portuguese's famous "Decree 77" was proclaimed in Angola a basic colonial policy was established. This decree forbade the missionaries to teach the seventy-five native dialects though they could still be used in all religious work and teachings. It was also required that all the new missionaries learn Portuguese, which is the reason my wife and I spent nine months in Portugal on our way to Galangue in 1923.

At first the missionaries were disturbed by Decree 77. They feared that it was aimed at closing down all Protestant work, but after they had had time to think the matter over, they called a conference and decided that a short course in Portuguese should be offered for all African teachers and for any missionaries who wanted to learn the language. A brilliant young Portuguese was put in charge of the school. He had studied in America. The school ran long enough to enable the teachers and missionaries to take the government examination which was about equal to our sixth-grade work, I would say.

We missionaries were not surprised that the Africans measured up as usual to the challenge. Some sixty of them passed the examination and the missionaries passed too, so our mission school could remain open. There was much rejoicing at the mission.

After that it was decided that all new missionaries coming to Angola should go first to Portugal for a course that went up to about seventh-grade work though it was more difficult because it was "foreign." Bertha and I were in the second group to be sent to Portugal for study, and we were much impressed by what we learned there. We were taught that the salvation of the natives was in our hands and we sailed into the strange new language with great vigor.

The general work soon settled down to normality again after the first impact of Decree 77 though from then on we knew and appreciated more of the Portuguese colonial policy, and the thought that lay behind it.

In my humble estimation Decree 77 turned out to be a blessing in disguise because prior to it the teaching throughout Angola was limited to each group and tribe. At Galangue missionaries could communicate with the natives only as they were able to learn and translate English into Umbundu. There was no common language or feeling between the different tribes as there is today, when the Portuguese language is common to everyone.

In modern times every two years or so there are held interdenominational missionary gatherings at which large numbers of Africans — deacons, preachers and lay workers from the various tribes — are present. With Portuguese the common language, they are able to converse among themselves and be understood. Also the common language brings the missionary and the Portuguese officials and teachers into a clearer understanding and enables us "foreigners" to appreciate the cultural background of our close neighbors, the Portuguese.

A common language is also advantageous to the Africans in that it gives them access to reading matter that is cheaper and better produced than that put out in their native languages. We have a number of students in our mission schools who go on with their education to the point where they can use and enjoy such literature.

When boys and girls finish the sixth grade in our mission station schools, they are sent to Dondi for four years of training. After completion of the course there, those who make the highest marks are chosen by the directors of the school for the government examination, given by the regional inspector of education. This examination is stiff, covering the work of our seventh grade.

Even to pass from one class, a child from the mission schools must be examined by the Portuguese. Examination is individual and sometimes there are fifty to one hundred spectators. But we never had to be ashamed of the Africans in our mission schools. They took the same examinations as the Portuguese children and in many cases made higher grades.

In order to raise the standard of teaching at Galangue and in the mission station schools, the church picked and sent scores of the best students to private Portuguese and government high schools for two and three years. When the young men finished those courses, they were given diplomas as government teachers. That increased their pay as well as their prestige. Some of these men are now operating grammar schools of their own, that have the same standard with the government as our mission schools.

Around 1933 Dr. McDowell, director of our mission, had the idea that Africans who had finished grammar school and lived on the same level as Europeans should be given some recognition. So he took the matter up with Portuguese officials. He was told that under the Portuguese laws such young men could apply for Portuguese citizenship and could vote. As citizens, they no longer needed to pay the native hut tax but only the military tax, which was cheaper. These are *Assimilados.*

Some missionaries looked upon this special privilege offered by the Portuguese with disdain and discouraged talented young men from applying, but little by little the idea became more popular. One obstacle to citizenship was the $30 to $40 cost of stamps and legal papers connected with the procedure, but once the idea became popular, the young men found the money somewhere.

The candidate for European status must be sponsored by a Portuguese administrator or two Europeans in good standing. A searching inquiry is made into his education and way of life. He must be a Christian and he must have given up the native African beliefs in animism and the practice of polygamy.

This legal standing has given those who have it poise and dignity. It is a recognition of their achievement, though of course it does not make Portuguese of them overnight, except in a technical sense. Most of the wise ones accept it as a badge, as they say. They can wear it and they can take it off — which is something the Portuguese must take into consideration.

I do not think that the actual certificate of "European civilization" is cherished by African natives so much as the knowledge that they are prepared through their industriousness and intelligence to meet the white man on his own ground and have been accepted as human beings.

Once a man has this status there is very little chance of his trekking off to South Africa, where a policy of segregation tends to build up a hostile community of great numerical superiority.

The Portuguese attitude toward the African native is that he must be taught and protected as if he were a child but accepted as an equal once he comes up to European standards. With four centuries of African experience behind them, they feel that their system is foolproof against unrest and the too rapid rise of African nationalism.

Today there is a Portuguese at each of the mission stations, sent there to teach his language. This is a good thing because he soon learns that we Americans are not there, for instance, to try to make Americans of the Africans. We are not an enemy in the Portuguese's midst, but a friend and cohort. There is growing up between the Protestant Churches of Portugal and the American and European Protestants a strong tie of brotherhood. That same feeling is growing between the native Protestant Church and the Portuguese, and also between the native Catholic Church and the Portuguese. For instance, there

are native African priests who preside over the white Portuguese Churches and at Lobito where they have a large
strong Catholic Church the assistant director of the church
is an African. This progress has come since the time of
Decree 77.

One man I could always hold up as an example of a successful Assimilado was Senhor José Mande of the county
of Quima. He got his start in the army, sometime in 1920,
as I recall it. Military service is compulsory with the Portuguese. The law applies to the Africans in Angola just as
it does to the Portuguese at home. But Senhor Mande had
a lucky break in the army. There he met one of the deacons of the Bailundu church who was able to read and
write in the native Umbundu language. The army officers
were allowing Deacon Jacob to teach the other soldiers
how to read and write and he also had religious services
with them on Sundays and at night.

Among about four hundred men in the detachment there
were only two books — the Book of St. John and a hymnbook — both belonging to Deacon Jacob. Those men were
as eager to learn as a ten-year-old boy is to go out and fly
a kite on a windy day, but there were only those two
books.

Without calling it that, those men decided to apply
the "each one — teach one" method, later reinvented and
popularized by the famous Dr. Frank Laubach. As a man
learned to read and write, he would copy a chapter of the
Book of John or a song from the hymnbook. By the time
some were discharged from the service, they had copied
the whole Book of John and every song in the hymnal.

They knew the Book of John just about by heart and could sing those hymns any time.

When Senhor Mande was discharged from the army, he returned to his village in Quima — the village of Mandi. Since he was able to read, write and speak Portuguese he could have obtained a job as an interpreter at the county seat of Quima without any trouble. Probably within ten years he would have been a rich man from the fees for settling natives' arguments out of court.

But seeing the needs of his people both from a spiritual and educational point of view, Senhor Mande cast his lot with the people of his village. As soon as he got back home his friends began to thrust tax receipts in front of him to be read. He was the only man in the county at that time who was able to read the names of the men on the tax receipts. Soon the natives referred to him as the Moses of his county because he had saved them from the Pharaohs — the Portuguese tax collectors. Two or three days before tax-paying time the men brought Senhor Mande baskets of eggs and carloads of pumpkins in payment for his services of just reading their names on the tax receipts, so there could be no question in the tribe as to who had paid and who had not.

But Senhor Mande was not satisfied with being the only man among 20,000 or 30,000 people who could read and write. So he began to teach others. He needed a school to make a good job of it, and to operate it he had to have permission from his local official. He asked to teach in the daytime and hold religious services at night and on Sundays. Permission was granted. Then and there the first church and school of Quima were established, through the efforts of a native who had pulled himself up by his own bootstraps.

Shortly after our Galangue mission was established in 1926, one Friday afternoon about three o'clock, Senhor Mande came to visit, leading about fifteen well-dressed men and women. He assured us they were able to read and write and had accepted our Lord and Master as their Saviour. They stayed with us at the mission and from among those early Christians of Quima came some of our strongest leaders.

Dr. McDowell made Senhor Mande a deacon of the Quima area and he built up there some thirty-three "bush school" and preaching places, with a central boarding school and a pastor who covers the whole county. When students of this central school finish the third grade, they take an entrance examination to the regular mission station schools.

After the village of Mandi had been made a part of the church of Galangue, Dr. McDowell sent one of his students to teach there during the dry season. He was Senhor João Carneilho. Senhor Carneilho was not afraid of the hoe. He soon became the leader of the people, both in the school room and on the farm.

Shortly after the Quima work had been started, I went along with two young men to put in an irrigation ditch for the teachers of the village and the people. This was the first time I had a chance to sit and have a good talk with Senhor Mande. I spent the night in his home and he talked to me as a brother. Since he seemed wide-awake, I told him that they should cultivate the rich river-bottom lands, and if they did they could get two crops a year from the same fields. He said he was willing to try. To give the idea a push I offered prizes to those at Quima who prepared the largest river-bottom field. A few months later, the valleys in the Quima region were a sight to behold. For miles there was nothing but newly broken ground. Senhor Mande was doing his work well.

Next came the plow. There was some doubt in my mind at that point about introducing the plow at Quima because some of the old men at Galangue had told me that the yoke was too heavy for their oxen, and I thought Senhor Mande might have that same outlook toward this animal that most people in the world consider a beast of burden, but for which the African has special consideration.

My approach to him was this: I told him, as I had told others, that by working his oxen, he would be saving the back of his wife, and that he would be growing twenty times more corn and beans. He was receptive. So I agreed to furnish him a plow for a year, train his oxen and teach him how to use it. When we returned to Angola from the United States in 1929 with our eleven plows, we earmarked one for Senhor Mande.

He brought over two oxen weighing about nine hundred pounds each that had never had even a rope around their necks. It was a job to catch them, but fortunately I had some drivers who were equal to the task. So after about two weeks of downright hard work the oxen were trained and Senhor Mande had learned to plow.

When the men of Quima county heard of this new back-

saving device that would "pull the hoe," they couldn't wait
to come and see how it worked. When the governor general of Angola visited Quima in 1937 there were over four
hundred plows in the county owned by the people.

When Senhor Mande and his family go to church, they
are well dressed. He has two sons who finished at our
Galangue school and went on to the central school of the
American and Canadian boards at Dondi. Their father
earned the money to pay their bills. The older boy today
is a registered nurse and has a good job with the railroad
at a salary more than that of the missionaries who gave him
his start. He serves not only the Africans but the white
people as well.

Senhor Mande does not push his company on the Europeans but they often invite him into their homes and to
sit at meals with them. He likes to brag that he does not
use palm oil to clean his body but has graduated to soap
and water.

In 1947 we held our general union church meeting in
Senhor Mande's village. When I finished a talk encouraging the natives he got up and said: "It wasn't so many years
ago that I used to put palm oil all over my body to make
myself beautiful, but when I'd go to a trader's place around
the noon hour, he would shut the door and push me out
until he finished eating. Now since I am able to raise corn,
and sell it, and dress well, comb my hair every day, wash
with soap, speak Portuguese and have a good bicycle, it
matters not what time of day it is. Always I am asked in
to have something to eat, or at least a cup of tea or coffee.
What I have accomplished any of you here can also do."

Even before the natives were granted citizenship, the work of the church and better trained leadership were on the upward march. There were thousands of young men who had completed grammar schools and were teaching and scores who had done two to three years of theological work, but prior to Decree 77 there was always a ceiling on a man's progress because of the lack of literature in the various African languages.

I know there are those who think it was wrong to put the natives into what they call the straitjacket of a single language, but looking at the present-day development of the people of Angola, I cannot share their pessimistic outlook. Today in Angola practically all of the railroad and telegraph operators are Africans. Gas station attendants are natives. Some are railroad conductors, stationmasters, truck and automobile drivers, mechanics, postal and railway mail clerks, foremen of all types, builders and cabinetmakers. A few have made the grade as bookkeepers, clerks in stores and one or two are outstanding businessmen.

I have seen Africans working in the custom houses as clerks and foremen, bookkeepers and revenue officers. About ninety-five per cent of these trained and educated young men got their grammar school training in some mission school, Protestant or Catholic.

There is no doubt that the Christian Church of Angola is fast becoming the outstanding factor in bringing together African tribes that for centuries were engaged in killing each other. Though there has been tribal raiding within the memory of almost all Africans, tribal warfare has been gone for half a century or more. The Portuguese put it down first by martial law but it was not until the Christians came that the softening process began which was to bring to the top the real peace and progress-loving side of the African natives. Today, knowing the benefits of education and the advantage of citizenship, the native is striving both day and night to reach these two lofty goals.

Grammar schools in Angola are maintained by the state. If an African speaks Portuguese and dresses well he is able to go along with the other children. There are only two or three government high schools in the colony. They prepare students for the universities of Portugal. When the Africans complete their high school work, if they have the money, they can attend the universities along with the other students.

In addition there are one hundred or more Roman Catholic schools in Angola. They are in part supported by the state and are for the teaching of natives, as a rule. A combined high school and seminary is located in Nova Lisboa. When a young man completes his high school work he then puts in three more years of work in the seminary. As a rule there are from forty to fifty young men attending the seminary and high school.

The Protestant missions of Angola have fifty or more mission station schools in Angola. There are six or seven different denominations at work. The American Board of Congregational Christian Churches and the United Church of Canada maintain a junior high school at Dondi, and a three-year seminary. The two missions also have a grammar school for girls and a hospital where both boys and girls receive training in medicine and care of the sick. The Methodist Church has a high school in Loanda and a seminary in Malange in the interior. The work done there is about the same as done in Dondi by the American and Canadian Boards. These denominations carry on regular grammar school work in all of their mission schools.

The central schools of Dondi are doing a little agricultural and industrial work, but it is very inadequate for the needs of just the area where they are working, to say nothing about the whole colony.

Today about eighty per cent of the Assimilados are Protestant. This is because we have carried on a wider scope of work for the natives than the Catholics. They have taken a few of the natives higher than we have but our program has been much broader.

At the last count, the number of "civilized" Africans in Angola had reached 30,000. That is less than one per cent of the people of the colony, so it is hard at this point to say what the impact of this banishment of the color bar for educated natives will eventually be.

It is a great thing for these young men of Angola to have the status of Assimilado to aspire to, but it is, in my estimation, even more important for them to have and know how to use the plow. With it they can really pull themselves and their families up and set them on the upward path of accomplishment which has no ending.

Listen to the story of Ebilo. In certain parts of Angola, not too many years ago, while domestic slavery was still practiced among the Africans unbeknown to the Portuguese officials, one day a young man named Ebilo and his sister Cecelia were out playing some distance from Galangue. Some carriers came by and caught them and took them away with the intention of taking them to the coast and selling them. But the Lord was with those children. As they passed through the Elende mission on their way to Lobito, Mr. Merlin W. Ennis heard the story and went out and intercepted the carriers and took the youngsters into the mission. The girl became a part of the Ennis household. She was bright. She finished school there and was sent to the central training school of the Congregational Boards at Dondi. She graduated there with honors in domestic science and other subjects.

But Cecelia remembered the area from whence she came. She made application through the Elende church to become a member of the Galangue church. This was granted. Cecelia came, studied nursing at our mission and married a nurse. They have a nice family now and their children are attending school and doing well.

Ebilo went through the Elende school and the central school at Dondi where he finished what is equivalent to about our sixth grade and then got a government license to teach. He taught just a few years, then got the fever to go to South Africa and work in the mines. He worked there three or four years, making good money, but he also came to the sad realization that he was looked down upon by the other natives owing to the fact that he came from the interior people who had no schools.

Ebilo made up his mind to go back to his home country to teach. The idea haunted him; finally he gave up his work in South Africa and came back to Angola. He came to the

Galangue mission and when we heard his story, we gave him work. He worked with us for two years and every so often he went out "itinerating" among his own people, the Vanyegamba. Finally he married a girl not of his tribe but one who was willing to go back with him to work among his people.

At that point the great hindrance in the way of starting this new work among a new tribe was money, but just about that time Mrs. P. S. Waterhouse of New Orleans and some of her friends gave us $50 for evangelistic work. We turned that over to Ebilo as salary for his first year's work. My wife and I gave him $5 and the Galangue church made some donations in the form of cloth, and he was on his way.

Dongo, which is literally a land "flowing with milk and honey," was ready to be awakened and Ebilo was certainly the man to do it. It was not long before carriers came back to us from Ebilo's station, asking for ten teachers whose salaries Ebilo himself was able to pay.

Ebilo speaks Portuguese and teaches it, under a Portuguese license. He is a bricklayer and he knows something about carpentry, and wants to inspire the people to get better homes. He has introduced the plow in Dongo. I always say the plow made its way there under cover of the Bible, but the fact remains it is there, and the economic revolution of the area has begun.

Another Assimilado who studied at the Elende school was Senhor Valeiria Buta. He was a bright young man. When Decree 77 came into effect saying that both the missionaries and Africans had to learn the Portuguese language, Dr. Ennis took two of his most brilliant young men and tutored them for their examinations. Many of the missionaries and Portuguese round about shook their heads. They said the boys would never make the grade. When the Portuguese examiners came, Buta and the other boy were presented by Dr. Ennis and both passed their examinations with distinction though they had never had any work under Portuguese teachers.

After that they went to Dondi for further training, spending four years in Bible training, pedagogy and so forth. Then they returned to Elende as teachers and preachers.

After some years, Senhor Buta decided that he wanted to return to his own country, Sambo, adjacent to the county of Galangue. He came to us at the Galangue mission, and we, seeing that he was a good teacher, used him as a night school teacher and director of the work at the Elombo farm.

During the two years Senhor Buta was at Galangue I talked to him often about agricultural extension work, in which he became very much interested, and he assisted me in carrying it out into the villages. We showed the people how to ditch their fields, how to break the valley land and how to work with the plow.

Senhor Buta then decided that he would open up a farm and school of his own at Kakalakasa, his home village. He commuted from Elombo for two years, bossing both places, but finally he settled down at Kakalakasa where he did magnificent work. He got wheat growing there and put the plow into use. He was the one who gave the

southern central part of Sambo its great send-off in the
wide cultivation of wheat. The Portuguese government
furnished the people all the wheat they needed to plant,
as well as corn and beans, and Senhor Buta showed them
how. The area around Sambo really became a center of
which traders were proud. They contributed financial and
other support to Buta's work which he had learned at the
Galangue station school. Today, in that area, the people
have plows and bicycles and are better dressed and fed
than most of their neighbors. The plow is the main element of stability there, showing that once it is established,
it will be a force for progress even if the people themselves
do some backsliding. The Assimilados should see that no
amount of pedagogy can give them the stability provided
by the plow. It will make it possible not only for them to
hold on to their status as Assimilados but will enable
them to put their children through school and give them
better homes and food, so they can go up higher. In other
words, the plow is the key to permanent progress in Africa
today.

The story of the life of the Reverend Jesse Chipenda
sounds unbelievable to most white men. He was one of
about fifty-two children. His father had so many wives
that it was hard for him to remember all of their names.
Even to survive among fifty brothers and sisters is quite
remarkable but Senhor Chipenda didn't stop at that.

When I first met him at Lobito in 1923, the Reverend
Jesse was in his early twenties. He was born of Ovimbundu
people in Bailundu in the interior of Angola. At an
early age he entered the Bailundu Congregational mission

school, where he showed considerable promise and ability. From there he was picked to go to the central school at Dondi. Upon graduation there he was chosen to take the government examination entitling him to enter junior high school. He passed with a high grade but instead of going on to the Portuguese school he was sent along with the late Dr. D. A. Hastings to work at Lobito among the Christian men and women of that growing city. Since the new mission there held services only at night and on Sundays, the Reverend Jesse had quite a bit of free time on his hands.

At that time the Pauline Construction Company, an English firm, was building large warehouses in Lobito. They needed a man of ability and honor to take charge of their large stocks of goods. The Reverend Jesse was chosen for the job. He did his work so well that he was soon given the keys to all of the warehouses which contained hundreds of thousands of dollars worth of goods.

As the native population of Lobito swelled, there was need for an elementary school for the children. The Reverend Jesse was sent to the government school at Loanda, capital of the colony, for a course that would entitle him to teach. Though he had been out of school for several years, he emerged at the head of a class of 90 European boys that included the son of the Governor General of the colony. Diploma in hand, he returned to Lobito, and opened up an accredited grammar school for the African natives. His pupils have all done well in competition with students from the regular Portuguese schools.

When Europeans began to attend the Reverend Jesse's

church services, it was decided that he should broaden his knowledge of the Bible so he was sent for a two-year course at the Dondi Theological School.

All the time Pastor Jesse had to supplement his salary by farming so he could make ends meet for his family. Even when he was made director of the whole coastal work, he got very little more pay. So he had to look to his "little hoe" for help.

Fortunately the Reverend Jesse had "given ear" to some of my talks at the annual mission meetings in Angola. Besides, every time I went to Lobito I talked to him about farming and how we Negroes in the States had worked hard to get ahead and get an education.

It was one of the Reverend Jesse's jobs to help traveling missionaries with their baggage and customs clearance. In May 1934, when we came through Lobito on the way back to America, I told Bertha I would like to give the Reverend Jesse something really worthwhile. "I want to give him a plow," I said. We had a little cash on hand from the sale of some household things and I bought the plow for $24 from Robert Hudson and Sons there in Lobito.

Jesse was deeply touched, but if I could have known then how far that little plow was going to shed its light I'm sure I would have been the humble one.

Twenty years later I heard from him that that "mother of plows," as he called it, had multiplied into forty-eight plows in his area. The men he had shown how to use the plow were gathering and selling as much as ten tons of corn. One man had paid $124 for an oxcart, others had bicycles, sewing machines and hand-powered gristmills.

The Reverend Jesse did not, as the Bible says, bury his talents in the ground. "I found a man who had four oxen and I joined up with him and we worked," he recalls. "Then all the others began to see. After two years I was able to buy three work oxen and my associate bought his own plow. I used the plow and the oxen in my speeches in special meetings. Thanks to God there are in that area now more than forty-eight plows!"

Two men in that area — João Caspinala and João José Ussuquila — used to live by hunting instead of farming. Many times their children had nothing to eat. Now each has two plows and enough cattle for work.

What the Reverend Jesse wanted more than anything else in the world was a wagon with rubber tires. The government would allow such a wagon to run on its dirt roads, and in it he could haul corn to Cabeça do Cão for himself and his friends. Corn that was then going to waste is now being sold there for $1.20 a bushel. He has worked twelve hours a day building roads and bridges. "With a wagon," he said, "I would help many as well as make money."

Today Pastor Jesse has his own wagon with rubber tires with which he is able to carry from ten to fifteen sacks of corn or beans to market on the government roads. On each trip of one or two days he realizes from $8 to $12. He has six oxen for his three plows and his wagon, and is anxious for more so when he is using his plows his wagon won't have to stand still. He will get these soon provided there is not a drought.

When he first began using the plow I gave him everyone

laughed at my friend just as they had at me. They said he was ruining the land, wasting his time and bringing suffering to the oxen. Now twenty-two of these same people have plantations of their own, with a total of 332 work oxen, 175 plows, two large wagons, 110 bicycles and 34 sewing machines! Some of those who previously lived by hunting have sold their guns.

One of the men who lived by hunting was Senhor Ussuquila. He never had cultivated a field larger than two acres and never had enough food for his family. Today Senhor Ussuquila has two fields containing fifty-one acres. When the rains are good, he gathers 600 to 700 bushels of corn, 350 to 400 bushels of beans, five to six tons of white potatoes and tons of other vegetables. He is one of those who have sold their guns. Senhor Ussuquila is doing well. He has two plows, six oxen, an oxcart, bicycle, a sewing machine and hand-powered gristmill for his wife. His children are in school.

The Reverend Jesse has permission from the government to build a blacksmith and carpenter shop but to build and equip it he will have to have some help. Such shops will be a God-sent blessing to the farmers.

That "mother of plows" the Reverend Jesse has now passed along where it can start to bear another family. "I gave that plow which is the mother of them all to a friend named Laureano Balur Chipeio," he told me. "I explained to him how I worked with the same plow. I think that God will be able to aid many with that same plow. Not that I don't like it any more. I still love it. I am going to speak to my friend about it and if he doesn't produce anything with it after five years, I will get it back again. If he works well with it, after buying his own, he will then give it to another person."

You can see that the plow has helped Reverend Jesse very much. "If it were not for this," he asks, "how could I pay for the school for my two boys, Daniel and Duarte? They go to school in Benguela and I pay $21.50 each month. My family spends $57 per month. I have to find $43.50 on the outside. This has been very difficult but God has given me the ability."

Again he wrote, "As you know, I have not had any course in agriculture, but our conversations have helped me a great deal. We have accomplished a great deal with the help of God and our good friend Coles who gave us the first plow." A little aid to a man with the will to succeed can sometimes produce amazing results.

It is commendable to know how to conjugate a Portuguese verb and become an Assimilado but to be able to dig a ditch or plow a straight row with a pair of oxen is even more crucial to the future of Africa.

10

Sleeping on the Subway

ONE OF THE first things that impressed me when I arrived in Galangue was the sight of thousands of oxen not being used by the Africans. Nor were the cows being milked.

I was only in the colony a few months when I made a vow to myself. I promised I would not give up the fight until every ox had bowed to the yoke, and until every cow in Angola had stood over a milk pail. That, I realize now, was quite a big task I outlined for myself. Maybe one man will not fulfill it in his lifetime but I like to think that by making it my guiding light in Angola, I have laid out a path toward a better life for the native people from which there will be no turning back.

My work in training oxen for the natives' use went along steadily almost from the time I arrived in Angola, but it was not until World War II came that I was able to do something about helping the natives learn to use the output of their cattle. When I came home to the United States at that juncture I made a beeline for Cornell University where

I enrolled in a short course in cheese making, to top off three years in practical dairying I had had while a student at Talladega College. At Cornell I made eighty-three pounds of cheddar cheese, working at times with my teacher until twelve o'clock at night to finish up a batch of this wonderful nourishing food that could mean a livelihood for many of my flock back in Africa.

There were nights then when I would dream about the natives and their cows. Those 3,500,000 cows counted in the 1940 census in Angola were indeed a formidable sight in my dreams.

Sometimes I would daydream too. I figured that those cows could average 1,000,000 quarts of milk per day and taking eight pounds of milk to make a pound of cheese, we would some day have 250,000 pounds of cheese per day in the hands of the natives. This would sell, I figured, for 30 cents a pound, which would mean a tidy sum in the pockets of the people who could make cheese. As it is, I do not believe there is a single pound of salable cheese made by the Angola natives, and calves are drinking down every year millions of dollars worth of milk that could be turned to money to educate the people.

I thought up other ways to help the Africans, too. You may not believe it, but in Africa today there are thousands of children who have stomach trouble every year because of the use of unsanitary eating utensils. I had brought home with me different types of Angola clay and had them tested in Trenton, New Jersey and at Alfred University in New York State. I was assured that one of them was kaolin, the key ingredient for high grade china. A bed of this clay is located only forty miles from my Galangue mission on a good road. This encouraged me to acquire the "know-how" for making some everyday things the rural African badly needs.

So after the cheese-making course was finished I sought out a good school of ceramics. I went to Alfred University and amazed the dean by telling him I wanted to take a "four day" course in pottery. I explained to him that I was a missionary working in Angola, Portuguese West Africa. He called in Dr. Charles Hardy, whose home was in my native state of Alabama, and when he heard my story, he agreed to take me in as a special student.

My first project was to cut down some forms for making common objects. The lathe that I was using ran perpendicular to the floor, hence when I wanted to shave off a little at the bottom of my work I had to bend my knees in a squatting position. I was told not to breathe or the chisel would "bite" my work.

The lathe was doing about 1500 r.p.m. and I was squatting but right away I had to breathe. The moment I did, my chisel dug into my work and the piece had to go to the junk pile. I worked at this three days, when, mind, I had thought I could finish the course or a least be an expert dishmaker in four days! Here I had just about flunked on my first project. I knew I needed to relax my whole body but I was not able to do it.

Then one night, while lying in bed, I thought of riding a bicycle. I realized that when I came to a stump in the road over there in Africa I did not tighten up, but just rode on as though the stump were not there. I tried out that approach to the lathe, relaxing there in bed.

At that moment I was so certain I had mastered that

lathe that I jumped up and dressed and went over to the ceramics building and my piece of work. With my whole body relaxed, I found I could just about finish a piece without having to take a breath.

My next project was mixing plaster of Paris. Dr. Hardy showed me how to do it. Here I was a model pupil and the whole class was called over to see how I could mix plaster of Paris without having bubbles in it. I said that anyone who could mix cake batter could mix plaster of Paris because the movement of the arm and hand were the same.

When I told the old men before leaving Angola that I was going to learn to make dishes, they pleaded with me, "Mr. Coles, please learn first how to make chamber pots for us because we are always catching cold having to go out at night." So the second thing I made, sure enough, was a chamber pot. After that I learned to make dishes with a machine, to make molds and to cast whatever I wanted to make from them.

One day in August 1943, sitting in my home in Jamaica, Long Island, I heard a man on the radio say, "Uncle Sam needs you if you are a blacksmith. Uncle Sam needs you!" I got to thinking about it and decided that if I did not answer that call I would be a slacker, so I put my cheese making and dish manufacturing into the back of my head and went down to the Navy Yard to help.

First thing they wanted to know was how many years I had run a drop hammer. I told them I had never seen one but was sure I could learn to run one in six weeks, but they wouldn't believe me. Instead, they sent me to the J.K. Welding Shipyard where I was hired as an anglesmith assistant.

That was a hot and heavy job, and because of my age, the men with whom I was to work told me I could not do it. Usually when the "big hammer" had to be used, Joe did it. He was a Jewish lad only thirty-two years old who weighed 160 pounds and was "the man" of the crew. Once Joe asked me if I could swing the hammer.

"Do you think a monkey can handle peanuts?" I retorted. I showed the men how to swing from the shoulders and it was not long before they were saying that there was only one other man in the whole shipyard among the 250 workers who could match my strength.

Still the desire to become an expert dishmaker for the Africans' sake kept nagging at me, so I entered the Barrow School of Art and Pottery in downtown New York at night. Three nights a week after a heavy and hard day's work in the shipyard I pushed, pulled and hauled myself across the river to Manhattan to learn to use the potter's wheel.

After three hours of school I would climb back on the subway train and usually fall fast asleep so the next thing I knew a guard would be telling me that we were at the end of the line. Then I would take the next train back and sometimes sleep two or three stops beyond my station. Then I had to wait a half hour in the cold for a bus and when I got home it would be well after midnight. In between times, I read up on the potter's wheel and the glory of the art.

It took me four or five weeks before I was able to center a piece of clay on the wheel so I could throw it properly. One night my teacher discovered the trouble. She came over to my wheel and scolded: "Mr. Coles, you are too soft with your clay. You must get hard with it." She took over and showed me how to be "hard." She grabbed, threw, squeezed and pushed it around a few times until it was centered and running true as a die.

From that night on, the potter's wheel and I became friends, though I never did get to the place where I could really sing to it.

As I worked I could just see those old African men with their chamber pots and their wives with tableware that would not be full of cracks where food could get caught and decay. Sometimes, too, I could even see African potters by the hundreds working away in their villages making dishes that they could sell to their neighboring tribes.

The men I worked with at the shipyard were very kind to me and held me in great respect when they learned why I slipped off at times to address dinner groups both in and out of New York. They seemed to understand when I told them that I was in search of knowledge wherever it could be found and was willing to pay a price. My work clothes were always hanging in my locker at the plant and sometimes I would return from a lecture outside of town just in time to slip into them before the work whistle blew.

Because of this full schedule, sometimes I did a little catnapping on the job, usually while the iron was heating. When the other boys saw the superintendent coming they would wake me up but one day I heard him say, "Don't wake him up." After that I really went to town with my catnaps, which kept me going at that hectic period.

As an anglesmith, my job was to bend iron for the ribs and plates which went into ships. I kept the job eight

months and learned much from Filippo, the Italian fore-
man. With what he taught me, I feel now that I am able
to duplicate almost any animal-drawn plow and the knowledge gained in that Brooklyn shipyard has been my mainstay in the development of heavy breaking plows in
Galangue.

In March 1944 I transferred to the Columbia Machine
Shop Works, Inc., as a helper on one of the large power
hammers. Soon I was shifted to bending links of chain for
the army. Though the work was hot and hard, I enjoyed
it because I knew I was picking up something new that I
could use in my work when I was able to go back to
Angola.

Here again the young fellows thought they would wear
me down because of my age but their respect increased
when they found I could keep pace right along with them
in the hardest kind of work.

In September 1944 I was sent out to Nebraska in the
interest of the work of the American Board of Congregational Christian Churches in Angola. At the machine shop
they were kind and allowed me to take the time off when
they heard what I was doing.

In Nebraska I kept my eyes open and for the first time
discovered the big factories which help to make America a
great nation. This, I told myself, was because everybody in
them worked. I saw, too, those great farms of the Middle
West. But the thing that impressed me most were the
cows in those sand hills of Nebraska which seem, at least, to
live on air, sunshine, sand and water. I did not see enough
grass to keep a goat alive, yet there were thousands of

head of fine cattle flourishing there on that arid land. It gave me new ideas and hope for Africa.

I was told that the cattle raised in those sand hills were sold to corn growers in the corn belt of the state and fattened by them for the market.

All through those Nebraska sand hills I saw small windmills pumping water for the cattle and homes. I examined them closely, telling myself all the time that some day I would make pumps and windmills for the cattle raisers of the Cunene River basin in Portuguese West Africa.

I visited the cattle ranch of the late Mr. C. C. Smith of Exeter, Nebraska, where cattle were being prepared for the market. My mind went out to the great African cattle raisers, and I thought: If only we as Christian workers could get the vision and teach the natives how to care for their cattle and get the best out of them, the way these midwestern Americans had learned to do!

When I got back to the machine shop I decided to try to make a pump, along with some skillets, pots, gristmill and Dutch oven. With that in mind I managed to get transferred to the foundry division, though I could only be paid as a common worker, 90 cents an hour, or $36 a week. When I was in the shop I had been making $85 a week, but despite the much smaller pay, the new job was worth it to me; I gained the knowledge I wanted. Once again there in the foundry I had to live down the idea that I was too old and too soft to do the work.

My first job was grinding and chipping the casting but shortly I was put with a young man who was a molder. There I ran smack into union rules for the first time. I was told I was not allowed to do any more than look at molding tools, because I was over age. The union trained young men from eighteen to twenty-two for that job, and being over fifty at the time I was out of the running.

But the idea of making pumps, wagon skeins and bushings for African oxcarts kept running through my mind.

I asked the superintendent of the foundry to allow me to mold at noontime when the men were not working. He said it would be all right with him but I would have to take it up with the union at one of the regular meetings. Anxiously, I presented my request. Although I was a member of the union I was not a molder, so I had considerable doubt in my mind that my plea for special consideration would be heard. All my hopes were shattered when the request was turned down, and my dream of making metal parts (I had even thought of casting church bells to replace the mournful horn the Africans use to call people to worship) looked as if it would never come true. I was terribly disappointed, but the union representative at the foundry advised me quietly to go in person to the next union meeting and ask permission to mold at noontime.

I went and stated my case as a simple Negro preacher. When I finished, every man in that room was shouting, "Let Coles mold." I broke down and cried, I was so happy.

I could see right then and there how that brief noontime instruction in the machine shop was going to pay off in good clean water, better means of transportation and better-cooked food for the African natives. I could see, too, how that knowledge was going to snowball into income that would enable my African friends to expand into simple industrial work.

Now that I had permission to mold things needed by the

Africans I faced the problem of getting patterns. For skillets and Dutch ovens I was able to copy items purchased at Montgomery Ward, but for the pumps and wagon skeins and bushings I had to have regular patterns and core boxes made. I went to a pattern office and asked what it would cost to make or purchase them. The reply was that it would cost about $200 to make the pattern and core box for the wagon skein and bushing. That was more than I had to spend.

One day a little while later, the director of the pattern office said to me: "Coles, if I were you I would take your pattern problem to the Pratt Institute here in Brooklyn, and ask their help. They will have students who can make those patterns for you, which will cost you much less."

At the Institute I was asked, "Why don't you come to night school and learn to make patterns yourself?"

So again I was going to school, enrolled in a course that covered the principles of patternmaking, bench and floor molding, coremaking, heat-treating of steel, forge practice, machine shop practice, electric and acetylene welding.

This meant four long hours a night, three nights a week, on top of my regular back-breaking job. At the time I entered the school I was assigned to charge the cupola at the machine shop. It consumed seven tons of iron per run and a ton of coke. This I had to tote from the yard in a wheelbarrow, load it on an elevator and stack it at the top. I put in two tons for the first charge, and when the fan was turned on and the men started pouring, I had to fast throw in another five tons within an hour. Believe me, that job required fast moving and a lot of elbow grease.

I got a book on charging cupolas so I could do a good job of it. Before I took over there had been five or six hundred pounds of castings rejected every day because the iron was not hot enough, but when I took over I am glad to say that I kept the iron at such a super-heat that there were never more than four or five castings thrown out each day because of cold-shots or holes in them. The men and the superintendent gave me a big hand for my work.

I handled about thirty tons of iron and coke a day, hauling, unloading, stacking and dashing it into the cupola. That plus twelve hours of night work at the Institute was enough to keep me out of trouble. Some mornings I would get home at one o'clock and have to leave again at five in the morning. At one point the snow was knee-deep as I waited for the bus to take me to work at that hour in the morning, before the plow had come through.

Always there were new obstacles to be overcome. When I finally got my patterns for skillets, wagon bushings and pumps, a Polish friend said flatly I was too old to learn to do foundry work. But I had a host of friends to teach me every day at noon. I plugged ahead. One day this Pole came to me and said he had decided I would someday be a "rich man out there in Africa." I am afraid this will never be true. That wasn't my goal. But I was at least pleased that he saw that with hard work, stamina and a steady goal one can achieve success at any age.

There were nights I felt very much like cutting class, but then I would figure out how much those hours might mean to the economic life of the African natives in the form of better transportation, cookware and better sources of water. From that I always took fresh courage and a new determination to go ahead with what I was doing.

On the side, I was still plugging away through speeches to various groups for new funds for the work in Angola. When I told people of my determination and the resulting long hours of study and new arts I was acquiring, many responded eagerly through the American Board. In July 1945 I attended a young people's conference in Green Bay, Wisconsin. Those young folks gave me $494 to buy twenty oxen to be trained at Galangue. There was one little lad there who only had $9, but he asked me to take it to "get a small ox and let him grow up."

After my three long years of hard work that kept me busy long into the night I finally felt I had prepared myself to help the natives of Africa in a practical as well as spiritual way. I went back to Africa with not only stars in my eyes but calluses on my hands.

The first job I had laid out for myself was the casting of some pots and skillets for those African folk, and I considered it an Act of God when I heard that two of my superiors, Dr. David M. C. Keith, Jr., Executive Vice President, and Dr. John A. Reuling, Secretary of the American Board, were coming to visit our mission in Africa.

I laid my plans for a demonstration of the work of the practical missionary very carefully. I had two projects in mind. First it came to me to build a natural-draft furnace, arrange a crucible and then cast a skillet and plowshare and forge a part of a plow.

Unfortunately the first skillet I cast had a hole in it because the metal got a little too cold, but the plow point, thank God, was perfect. I was praying and my heart was in my mouth but when we "shaked out" the first thing I saw was a plow point without flaw. I could not keep back the tears, so moved was I to be able to show what could be done by a humble missionary there in the jungles of Africa.

Imagine my deep disappointment, then, when after my demonstration was over, Dr. Reuling took me aside and told me I must confine my work to the making of parts for plows, and the making of tiles. He was also in favor of developing blacksmithing and wheelwrighting and, of course, agricultural work, but he thought it was too advanced for me to try to make plows.

Just before our visitors left Angola I received a letter from Dr. Reuling saying, "Sam, forget about foundry work." What a shock! I thought back over the eight months I had spent in that Brooklyn factory and all those hours I had put in improving my studying and here it looked as if I was not going to be able to cast even such a little thing as a skillet.

Once again I turned to the Master. I knew I had to be obedient and concentrate for the time being on bricklaying, blacksmithing and farm work, but I was also confident that all those things I had learned in behalf of the African native after living beside him and analyzing his needs would some day come in handy. I knew I must bide my time.

II

Welfare and Warfare

FOR THIRTY YEARS I have been chiefly an "apostle of the plow" in Africa. During that time I have given some deep and serious thought to the great opportunities there for trade development.

Probably Angola's products seem secondary in importance to people sitting in Washington but I know from my experience serving with the Board of Economic Warfare in World War II how they can suddenly become prime. One never knows when one will need the friends he makes during long non-emergency periods.

My contact with Washington began with the discovery of some unusual leguminous plants in Angola in 1936. I thought the Department of Agriculture would be interested, and went in person, bearing twenty-three of them, when we came home at the outset of World War II. I found government officials at that time more interested in winning the war than in plants that might improve agriculture over a long period of years, and before I knew it I was snatched up by the Board of Economic Warfare as an adviser on Africa. Having traveled widely in Africa myself and having talked to many people who had covered the ground even more extensively, I was able to name right off several items which Africa was then producing which the United States needed. If Hitler should take over Africa the only way to get them would be through Germany. That was a grim prospect but not an impossibility. The men I worked with during those six months in Washington were deeply concerned about the outcome of the war and its relation to Africa and its people.

Among the items Angola was called upon to supply the Allied Nations armies during World War II were tinned fish, coffee, beef and sisal. Linton Wells, the author, was sent to Angola to buy up those commodities for the Allies. I was called to Washington chiefly because of some information I gave on the production of sisal which was needed for sandbags. Today we are still importing this product from Angola by the thousands of tons to make ropes and cord and also corn and wheat sacks.

During my stay at the Board of Economic Welfare, every ton of freight which went to Angola had to have my OK before it could be sent and I had to look back three years to see how much of this item Angola had imported. If the order was greatly enlarged over what Angola had been importing we cut it down. We did not want strategic goods to leak through neutral Portugal to our enemies.

One day a commercial firm of Angola placed a large order for dried milk in the United States. It was so much larger than previous orders that we suspected some of it might get to Germany. Here my experience and knowledge of the Africans came in handy. I took the bull by the horns and canceled the whole order, saying to myself it was high time that Angola with its tremendous number of cattle should put aside its taboos and begin teaching the natives how to milk.

I studied the roads and railroads of Angola before orders were filled for reinforcements and I made all kinds of subsidiary studies that might come in handy in defense connected with things I knew about the Africans, such as how castor oil could be used as fuel in trucks for short hauls, prospects of growing rice in Liberia and how salt could be manufactured more widely in Africa so our ships would not have to be used to take it from the States to our soldiers.

Finally the Board of Economic Welfare was convinced that Angola offered vast commercial advantages to the United States and I was ordered to make a survey of its commercial houses and compile facts that would be of use to American exporters. I was glad to do this both for the sake of my own country and for the natives among whom I had worked so long. Shortly after my tabulation was made, every commercial firm of any note in Angola had received a request from some American business firm asking it to become its agent. Today there is not a store in any of Angola's cities that does not carry some American-made goods. You can even buy American-made sun glasses.

Angola is still primarily an agricultural country. That is because the natives have not yet found a way of licking the problem of mere subsistence. The natives have a few cash crops such as sisal, coffee and sugar, and these have found a ready market both in Europe and America and I predict the day will come, and soon, when there will be more interest among the Africans in the earning of money.

A study by the United Nations has shown that in Africa as a whole about 70 per cent of the land and 60 per cent of the labor is still engaged in mere subsistence production. The Gold Coast has 70 per cent of its cultivated land and labor resources commercialized but that is quite exceptional.

The main commodities that are exported out of Angola today are corn, beans, wheat, rice, wax, hides, skins, sugar, salt, cattle, and a little cotton and manganese. Considering the extensive natural resources of the area that is not a good showing.

Lack of transportation is one of Africa's fundamental problems. Today, generally speaking, people who live more than two hundred miles from a railroad produce only enough corn and beans to pay their taxes and get a few yards of cloth or a couple of cheap blankets for their families. There is no incentive to do more. If they had ox-carts to haul their corn and beans to the railroad or to the truckline, then they would be able to produce thousands of tons of exportable crops every year.

There is a section up in the county of Dongo, on the Cunene River, about one hundred miles from its head, that has been called "the Canaan of Angola," yet its great abundance is wastefully used and largely thrown away today.

In this "promised land," honey flows like water. Milk is there in abundance all the time. The Varyamba people are great cattle raisers and, unlike most Angola natives, they milk their cows and make a lot of butter. You can tell a rich man's wife in Dongo long before you get to her by the smell of rancid butter. They have so much, they rub themselves with it.

During the honey season the Portuguese traders buy as much honey as they can find containers for and they buy all the beeswax the natives can produce. The present methods of producing the honey are primitive and uneconomic. Crude hives are put in the trees to collect the wax and then they light fires to drive away the bees, which perish in large numbers. Sometimes the natives just go out and hunt for nests of bees in trees and on finding them kill the bees, often cutting down the trees. I have been told that in Dongo when the natives have filled their containers and can't find anyone to buy the loose honey, they take it to the river and dash it into the water and wash the honey out, sweetening the water for the fish.

Wax could be produced in a continual stream if African extension workers were trained in bee culture and if the native boys were taught to make hives.

At one time rubber was the most important export crop of Angola but today it plays a minor role in the economy. Rubber grows wild in the forest region of the county and is particularly abundant in the Luanda district. A rapid decline in rubber prices came about when production was stepped up in Malaya and the Netherlands East Indies. Angolan rubber could not compete, chiefly because it was poorly handled. I am convinced that the rubber industry could be revived today without too much trouble if trading centers were established with machines for washing and reprocessing the rubber and the natives were offered guaranteed prices and markets until they got started again.

Rice growing was introduced about thirty-five years ago in Angola. The government has not particularly encouraged its cultivation but there are many regions in Angola well adapted to this crop. Approximately half of the interior is suitable for rice growing and all the coastal region could grow swamp rice.

On one of my early trips home to the United States I had learned how to plant and raise swamp rice. I knew that it had done well three hundred miles north of us in the state of Bie where it was introduced by the late Reverend William C. Bell, an American Board missionary, and also further to the south of us in the Elende mission. The type they raised was dry-weather rice. I wanted to know something about the cultivation of swamp rice. So I went to Homer, Louisiana, and to other parts of that state to learn.

I found they let rice, weeds and grass grow together until they are ten or twelve inches tall. Then the whole field is cut down to within three or four inches of the ground. After that the field flooded and the water stands in the field six or seven inches deep. The water kills the grass and weeds but helps the rice to grow.

In the fall of 1930 I got 400 pounds of red rice from Dr. Merlin W. Ennis of the Elende mission. I planted about half of it myself and the rest I distributed among the native farmers. I gave one man 24 pounds and he gathered 648 pounds. He cultivated rice for several years, there on the border of Galangue and the county of Dongo.

A few years ago the Portuguese gave the farmers of Dongo some rice and today there is a large rice-hulling plant at the county seat of Dongo, which is stimulating rice growing both as an aid to the food supply and as a cash crop for the natives.

My knowledge of swamp rice growing came in handy during a trip I made to the Quanyama country in the southern part of Angola. While there we went over on the English side, known as Ovamboland, to visit some Finnish missions. We went by to see the local official and I raised the question of food for the people in this semi-desert country. When there was rain there was usually too much; ideal conditions for rice, and I told them all I knew about how to cultivate it.

We left Angola in December 1940 on our furlough and I did not know how the experiment came out until 1947 when I drove three hundred miles from Galangue to Ovamboland to find out whether they were growing rice, and they were. However, they were having some difficulty in the hulling of it, which they tried to do with a mortar and pestle, which cracked the rice. It is too bad they do not have the simple hand-powered rice hullers that are available.

Not only will rice make a welcome and nutritive addition to the diet of the African people, but if they have machines to hull it and a system of transportation is opened up to them, it can be made a lucrative crop for the whole colony.

I would like, too, to see castor beans grown more widely as a commercial crop. At present they are treated too casually. When plants come up in their cornfields, or around their homes, the natives gather the beans and sell them in exchange for salt, dried fish, palm oil, soap or buttons. Only a few people gather enough to be sold for money now, but I am convinced that with a conducive price and guaranteed tonnage, production could reach 25,000 to 30,000 tons within a few years time. If equipment for extracting and processing the oil could be made available, that would add new impetus to the production because processing on the spot would reduce the bulk in shipping and automatically enable the buyers to pay better prices to the natives.

The whole coast of Angola will produce coconuts but at present the output of copra does not represent the full productive capacity by any means. If a good price were guaranteed and trading centers established in strategic areas, the output could be doubled within just one season. It takes a coconut palm five to six years before it starts to bear, but in the meantime the same land can be planted in rice, beans and bananas and in this way the land will be kept clear of weeds, grass and bushes, and nitrogen will be added to the soil.

The same general principle used in cultivating coconuts can be applied to the palm plants from which palm oil and palm kernels can be obtained. Here again it would take only a single season to produce a big surplus crop if the Africans were paid a better price and furnished machinery to crack the kernels so the oil can be extracted.

In 1936 the Reverend R. S. Webb of the American

Board Mission at Bailundu gave me a piece of metallic rock which was brought up by an African digging a ditch. I took it home with me and had it tested at Tufts College. The test showed it was seventy-six per cent copper. I know of another deposit of ore that was found in 1926 by some American missionaries who built a mission station in the south central part of the district of Bie. When the government learned the copper was there, the mission station had to be closed. There are also said to be rich copper deposits in eastern Angola, adjacent to the Katanga mines in the Belgian Congo. These resources probably could not be exhausted for many years, but to make the copper of any use smelters would have to be erected at the mines. The ore could be reduced with hardwood charcoal at not too great an expense.

The fishing industry has grown rapidly since my early days in Angola. Today there are nearly 2000 fishing vessels registered with the government. Fishing centers are at Luanda and at Mossamedes further to the south. If Angola fishermen were assured of a good market, they could probably be ready to export more than 10,000 tons of dried fish within a year.

Nobody knows exactly how many cattle the Africans have because they never declare them all to the officials, but the number has been estimated at as high as 2,000,000. Some individuals have as high as 14,000 head.

This great potential resource could even be expanded, for at present about 20 per cent of the grown cows and 30 per cent of the calves die each year. The calves die of intestinal parasites, lice, mange and ticks and the cattle die mostly of lung disease.

The Portuguese government has three or four veterinarians, but with a small subsidy a veterinarian school for Africans could be opened in the colony. If this were done I am sure that cattle raising would increase something like 50 per cent in ten years time. If the milk capacity of both the cows and the goats in Angola could be harnessed, the colony could be made to export 50,000 tons of cheese annually, I am sure, to say nothing of other milk products.

Before an attempt is made at hog raising on a large scale in Angola there will have to be a vaccination drive against cholera because at present there is a cholera epidemic every three or four years. For several years I conducted a pig club in our villages. I gave the men a good breed of pigs and they did quite well. If we could get rid of the disease by vaccinating, it would be easy to revive pig clubs in the villages for both boys and girls.

At present the government has two experimental stations in cattle breeding in Angola. One is located at Ganda on the Benguela railroad about one hundred miles from Benguela. The other is at Humpata, ten miles from Sá da Bandeira which is on the Mossamedes-Sá da Bandeira Railroad. These two breeding centers are well managed. They are equal to some of the best in the United States. Their experiments have been carried on with the leading breeds of European cattle. These crossed with the cattle of Angola have achieved some amazing results. Some of the third and fourth crosses give as much milk as the European breeds. By sending several thousand European bulls to Angola, herds of hundreds of thousands of cows can be built up and shipped to Europe within about ten years, and this program may be enlarged.

At one time a market in beef was established with the mother country, but all the meat the Portuguese were able to produce was tough, and the trade soon dwindled. Efforts must be made to raise the quality of livestock and better refrigeration facilities are needed.

The tanning industry would be another desirable and feasible development in Angola. Mangrove bark, which contains tannic acids, can readily be obtained in large quantities from Portuguese Guinea for use in the processing of Angola hides.

You can see that Angola is a country of considerable agricultural and mineral potentialities. It ranks third among African countries in this respect but today less than one per cent of it is under cultivation. That includes a small portion farmed by European concessions.

If the United States is interested in developing these markets I would suggest that it give attention to five points: (1) a regular and sufficient outlet for materials produced; (2) improvement of present transportation facilities; (3) adequate incentives to native producers in the form of higher prices and better goods for trade; (4) equipment for the primary processing of agricultural and industrial raw materials, and (5) a more efficient system for collection and storage of produce.

It would be well for us to remember that for a while during World War II German interests operated successfully in Angola and that the Nazis widely penetrated the Angolan economy. The axis was thus able to obtain critically needed materials from Angola through Portugal, which caused a great deal of concern in Washington. I was on the scene in Washington and I know, though fortunately we had the necessary money at hand so we could outbid the enemy on the Portuguese market most of the time. There was a special need at that time for sisal for sandbags, though a wide variety of produce was needed to supply the large number of Allied troops serving in the African campaign.

At present the heavy outflow of labor is also affecting the native agriculture. It is quite evident that as economic development proceeds, more and more people and resources will move into local industry, but quite apart from that is the loss that is already occurring by the movement of our people off the land into the cities of South Africa.

We must give them more incentive to stay on the land where they belong. That is where I have come in and I hope other missionaries and government folk will come in. The new International Finance Corporation which is to be set up by the United Nations to lend to backward areas where there are greater financial risks than the World Bank is able to handle may help. I hope so.

Africa can expect great things, too, from the application of President Eisenhower's atoms-for-peace proposal. The possibilities of atomic research are certainly vast and although it would be unwise to expect too much tomorrow, radioactive tracers have already shown that it is sometimes possible to improve soil fertility and expand productive areas.

If research proves that this can be done in areas where recurrent crop shortages are a major concern, it might one day open the way to agricultural prosperity. Who knows?

I understand that radioactive tracers have also been used successfully to combat the destructive effects of insects and blight. This would certainly be a tremendous blessing to Angola. What it would mean in the way of improving crops for export is hard to exaggerate.

I consider it a problem for the whole world that Africa's crop yield is at present the lowest in the world. It needs at least to be doubled.

One day in Freetown, West Africa, I was pleased and surprised to find a native friend of mine reading a catalogue from Hampton Institute, the well-known institution of higher learning for Negroes at Hampton, Virginia. I was surprised because those few local people who could afford to send their sons out of the country to school had usually sent them to England. It seemed to me a good sign that this man was thinking of Hampton, where practical skills are taught: too many graduates of English universities, when they come home, merely hang up their diplomas and sit around expecting to be waited on as they have been at Oxford or Cambridge.

The Africans are beginning to realize that what they need are people who will roll up their sleeves and go to work. It is appalling to me that though there are many doctors of economics, not one orange or one banana is being shipped by the blacks out of our part of Angola today.

The people need to be taught quality and they need to be taught cleanliness. Three fourths of the world's cocoa is being shipped out of the Gold Coast and Nigeria today and there is no reason why Angola should not share in that trade, but thus far the colony has been unable to meet the high standards of cleanliness set by such people as the Swiss.

The natives will have to do their part in learning the right way to do things. I have tried to impress on the people that if a sow has twelve or fifteen piglets and can't care for more than five, the whole litter will starve. So, too, if they throw four or five grains of corn into one hole, they won't get anything worth while. But if they will work and weed out all but two grains, then they will have two big stalks.

My ideal of an African Christian village would be like a typical New England town. The church should set the tone for all the work that goes on. It should not be an end in itself. We should furnish a community center where both the Portuguese and the native leaders could be invited in to discuss community problems. The Portuguese could utilize the leadership that these old folks already possess. We should be capitalizing on this situation instead of ignoring it. Too often the attitude of the church is "You're just an old devil. You must recant before we can have anything to do with you," and this rigid attitude toward the tribal elders merely alienates the one group that has real influence among the people. At the same time, the African has got to be taught that he can't just "cuss" his way through his problems. He has really got to buckle down and work through them. That's all there is to it.

Most Africans today live in villages where they originally went for security. All of these today could stand a little city planning. Undoubtedly the old "stick and dirt" buildings will continue to serve the Africans for many years to come, but if streets could be laid out and an elementary form of water sanitation introduced, the people would begin to move forward. The villages need to have talks on health, better methods of farming, livestock improvement, and citizenship.

In times of drought, simple lessons about the planting of English peas — that will grow even during the worst dry season — and other emergency programs could save hundreds of lives.

I hope to see the day when we can introduce that great American institution — the county fair — into Africa. It would do much to inspire the people to simple improvements. I can envision a great transformation of the African village just in my lifetime.

Sometimes when the Africans protest against my making them work so hard, I tell them they are building a great building — that is Africa. Right now they are at the stage when they must throw a lot of rocks into the foundation. It is hard work and nobody can see what the building is eventually going to look like. When they start to build the superstructure then they can hew their rocks carefully and face them with brick, but it is the foundation that counts. It will be supporting the whole building. Later on they will see the beauty. I keep repeating my byword "ka chivala ka chikuete ondando," — "That which doesn't hurt, it hasn't any value."

It's not just a question of teaching the native to work harder, though that is part of the whole picture. But all the time he has to be shown how he can produce more with the same amount of labor. That means he has to have more to do with. That is what the missionary doesn't very often think of.

When you speak to the average well-trained missionary about "technical training," his mind usually flies off to engineering or some other field way above the average African. That's because the average American doesn't think of a wheelbarrow or a blacksmith's forge as "technology." But they are, as far as the African is concerned. The missionary, even if he agrees with you about the necessity of more Point IV work connected with the missions, is apt to go out to his post with a whole lot of hifalutin ideas and equipment put out by Uncle Sam that doesn't meet the Africans' needs at all.

The frustrated American will soon find himself about as badly off as the natives. If he doesn't know their language he will say the people cannot learn. You can be pretty certain that he won't know how to get into a ditch and put in a drainage system out of the rocks and logs at hand. Yet our forefathers did that before drainage tile was ever invented. *

It's all very fine to preach "progress" to crowds of five hundred to a thousand people, but when ninety-nine per cent of them have lice and no soap, it seems something of a practical nature should be done about it.

At present it takes the African a week to cut an acre of wheat because he has no adequate scythes, yet any blacksmith can make these. But somebody has to train the blacksmiths.

In Angola today there are millions of acres of rich bottom land that has never even been crossed by an African.

The African sits and waits until the white man gets the idea of turning these fields into living, producing assets, and we just sit and wait too.

At present the African who wants to keep his fields productive has to carry his compost on his head. He has none of those three-wheeled wheelbarrows you see around every farm in America. I know men in Africa who, if they had a wheelbarrow, would push their corn seventy-five miles to a hundred miles to market. At the present time, with the 75-pound legal limit to the amount a man is allowed to carry on his back, it doesn't pay to carry only that small amount to market if the distance is great. A wheelbarrow in which one man could carry 200 to 300 pounds would begin to change the whole economy.

Listen to my friend Jesse Chipenda and you will begin to understand the great hunger for a better life that motivates many Africans today.

My wife and I work constantly most of the time. We never think of taking a rest [he wrote me not long ago]. *Our time is taken up with the work of the church and the rearing of our children so that they will be useful members of society. My salary is not sufficient for the education of our children, but God has given us health, strength and wisdom to till the earth from which we can reap an abundant harvest. We dig the ground to get our food and lift up our eyes to the Lord to get His Grace.*

In 1953 I asked the church to allow me to remain in the area in which I was farming for a few months in order to open up a longer highway and build needed bridges. After much talking with the people of that area, telling them of *the advantages of good roads and bridges, I worked with them and we lengthened the highway and built seven bridges. I worked like this 12 hours a day for four months. All the people thought that after doing so much manual labor for such a length of time I would be sick and perhaps die, but with the help of God my health remained good. When all my work was completed I called a truck of the trader to whom I sold my corn for which I was paid $408.*

Most people cannot even imagine what a God-sent blessing the oxcart is to an African. With an oxcart the man of the family hauls wood and water for use in the house and he carries his farm produce to the market with it. Without it, his wife, his daughter and he would all be common carriers, toting their corn and beans to the markets fifty or more miles away.

Of course the objection may be raised that these are "material things." They are, but they have their place in the present-day life of Africa, along with the word of God.

Africa needs many hundreds of beds. Hundreds of cabinetmakers, masons, carpenters, wheelwrights, blacksmiths and shoemakers could find work. If there were opportunities at hand to learn, there would be no need for the young men trekking off to the cities looking for better paying jobs.

Black Ivory

AFRICA's call for help has always been sharp in the ears of the American Negro.

As early as 1834, a Mr. Thomas Keith, an emancipated slave who remembered being taken from his home on the Niger River of Nigeria, is reported to have worked his way back to his homeland where he served as a missionary for several years. This humble servant of God carried a tattered letter of recommendation from his pastor, but no money. He had no budget and no salary. He was sustained by his faith in the Master and the joy he knew would be his from working for his people.

The Amistad Mutiny in 1839 wrote a new chapter in the history of missionary work of the Congregational Church in America. A group of African slaves mutinied on a ship that was taking them from one Cuban port to another and brought their ship, the Amistad *Friendship*, into port off Montauk Point, Long Island. When the court finally set the Amistad mutineers free, the men were restless and wanted to go home. Among the missionaries found who were willing to go with them were a Mr. and Mrs. Williams who were colored. They went to Freetown, West Africa, and opened up what was known for many years as the Mendi Mission.

The first record of missionaries being sent to Africa under organized auspices was when William Knibb, an English Baptist missionary to Jamaica, got together a shipload of forty-three men, women and children in 1843 and sent them off for Africa. They landed on the island of Fernando Po, in February 1844, where they were well received by the natives. But since the slave trade was still being carried on, they were soon considered a disruptive influence by the Spaniards and had to move along to the Cameroons.

During those early years of missionary work in Africa when the slave trade was still flourishing, it was like Daniel walking into the lion's den for the American Negro missionaries, but during those years, thanks to God's protection, there were no charges brought against any missionaries of color by colonial officials for trying to incite the Africans into rebellion.

The Negro missionary of those days could see and hear the lash of the slave trader, and see heartrending starvation on all sides, but he did not lay himself open to hatred and resistance from local authorities. He was not thinking in terms of political freedom but of freeing the mind, spirit and soul, and of relieving the body of disease and hunger. He was doing God's work and he knew it. He knew, too, that when these freedoms were achieved the rest would follow as surely as night followed day. He set himself quietly and steadily to the task of educating the people, teaching them trades and imparting to them principles of Christian living.

Having been just freed himself from the horrible yoke of slavery, the American Negro was well prepared to take up the hard "spade work" as missionaries among the people of Africa. When the opportunity to serve presented itself, they were never found wanting.

Space does not permit me to give all the names of Negroes who have served in the missionary field in Africa and the records are hard to come by, but I can tell of some of those I have known or known about.

In May 1894 a Dr. and Mrs. William Sheppard sailed for the Belgian Congo under the auspices of the Southern Presbyterian Board. I know about her because she had graduated from my college — Talladega — and he from Stillman Institute, of Stillman, Alabama.

They had a honeymoon trip of 10,000 miles and were royally received in the heart of Africa. They were treated to "dried rats, corn meal, eggs, chickens and caterpillars."

The darkness and ignorance they found was appalling. After Mrs. Sheppard had been there only a few days, she saw the condition the people were in and overnight became head nurse, domestic science teacher and schoolteacher. When she established her schoolroom she discovered that no one knew a single letter because there were no books in the whole area. She set herself to the task of not only writing the first book, but of making a dictionary to go along with it.

The Sheppards' first stop was at Léopoldville, then they

pushed on for another 263 miles to Luebo, where they helped to found and develop the great work of the Southern Presbyterian Board at that place.

Dr. Sheppard was ever on the lookout for new work and new people. So he went and spent a year with a new tribe — the Bakubas. After a year among the people, Dr. Sheppard built a home for Mrs. Sheppard and she became the first American woman to visit that part of Africa. When she saw the native women with their nearly naked bodies covered with oil, she didn't think there was much she could do for them, but it was not long until she had begun to change their lives. She finally had those African women working as missionary leaders, caring for the sick and helping with the general churchwork. Certainly the early history of the missionary work of the Congo cannot be written without the name of Dr. William Sheppard. He played a great part in breaking up the slave trade among the natives and in planting the Christian Church among the Africans.

Reverend A. L. Edmonston of the Southern Presbyterian Church was knighted by the Belgians for the great service he rendered to the Congo. When I visited there in 1946, both Africans and missionaries told me of the great service he had rendered as a teacher, preacher and farmer. I think he was the first to grow watermelons in the Congo.

When the Congregational Church of America and Canada opened their work in Angola in 1880, a colored man, the Reverend Mr. Samuel Miller, went along with two whites. At that time the Portuguese government did not have the country under control and when the party arrived in Bailundu the tribal king didn't like their looks and asked them to leave the country. They returned to the coast by which time the king sent runners to bring them back. He had changed his mind. But the Reverend Mr. Miller had returned to America.

Missionary authorities in America still had faith in the Negro as a missionary to Africa. They sent the Reverend and Mrs. D. A. Hastings to Angola. They worked a while in two or three of the mission stations, then were sent to Bailundu where they stayed for about twenty years. They built the finest native church anywhere around. Today it boasts the largest membership of any Congregational Christian Church in the world. When Dr. Hastings retired in 1938, membership was around 10,000 with 500 or 600 teaching and preaching. All of the church's work was interracial and peace and good fellowship was the prevailing rule among the mission station workers. Dr. Hastings achieved a superb relationship with both the Portuguese officials and the Africans, which he maintained right down through the years.

Just before we went to Africa a Dr. and Mrs. Reuben S. Hall of Jamaica, B.W.I., were sent out to Angola by the Canadian Congregationalists as medical missionaries. They were there only five years but left good footprints upon the hearts and minds of the Africans and Portuguese. Dr. Hall was a graduate of McGill University, a school teacher and a graduate pharmacist.

Upon arrival, Dr. Hall began daily to see cases which needed to be operated on but he could not do it because there was no hospital. The Women's Board of the Canadian Congregational Church gave him $5000 for a hospital and equipment, and in May 1924 at the Chissamaba mission a new spacious hospital was dedicated with an operating room and all the "trimmings." Dr. Hall soon won the admiration of both the natives and Portuguese, though he had been warned that Africans would not even sleep in hospital beds. He said he didn't want them to. He merely wanted to give them a chance to get up and get out.

A new chapter in interracial work for the natives of Africa was started in 1923 when our mission at Galangue was opened. Some people feared our station would be only a "fifth wheel" in the Congregational missionary work in Africa and others said we would cause trouble between the natives and the Portuguese government, but neither of these dire predictions has come true.

All of us, coming from the southland of the United States where our race was being given a chance to rise from the ravages of slavery, knew that with education combined with the Word of God the Africans would be able to work out their own destiny with the whites in Angola. Our job was to give them the tools.

Our Point IV work may seem crude when it is compared with some of the big government programs today but it was right down at the people's level. Though there naturally had to be a good deal of improvising, we gave the people what they needed.

For instance, there was the domestic science work that my wife carried on among the women of the mission village. It followed in general the "housekeeping" course Booker T. Washington said they were teaching the girls at Tuskegee — cooking, patching, ironing and washing.

Most of the poor people we dealt with had never had but about half a change of clothing. In the evening, Bertha

would take a light and along with a dozen or more women
from her domestic science class go to one of the homes.
First they would clean it from top to bottom to show what
good housekeeping was like. The next week all the women
would bring along something to cook and they would go
to another house. The husbands would be asked to come
in to sample the food. The benefits were twofold. Not
only did the women learn to cook better, but after that
their husbands were willing to work harder so there would
be more and better food to cook.

Saturday night was usually patching night. The poor
women would wash everything they could find which
would hang together and bring it along to be patched.
Sometimes the patch was bigger than the garment, but
that didn't matter.

Sometimes the women would be able to buy cloth
enough to make a child's dress. Then Bertha would show
them how to cut and sew the garment. There are plenty of
women in Galangue today taught to sew by her who can
keep up with their daughters trained at our Central School
for Girls.

When Bertha and I returned to Angola after World
War II, she reorganized the school work. We got a Portuguese colored girl to take charge of preparing the young
men for the government's sixth grade examinations. These
young men were teachers and had families. They were
getting $8 a month, and had been implementing their
salaries by working in the fields Saturdays and afternoons.

Actually those young men needed both the extra training as well as the food for their children. How could that
be arranged?

I pitched in and gave them a few pep talks on work and study. They took me at my word. They rolled up their sleeves and went to work. True, it took two or three of them two years to pass the examinations but then they were able to go on to the regular Portuguese junior high school, and the extra "umph" they learned to put into their work paid off in many ways. First, the quality of their teaching improved. Second, it showed a lot of people around Galangue what could be done if they had the will power to try it. Today, every one of these young men has his own plow and bicycle. They have better homes and have attained Portuguese citizenship.

I have felt it necessary to give this report even though it may sound a little self-satisfied, because today for some reason there are fewer Negroes working in Africa under our interracial church denominations than ever before. I don't know quite why. I have asked many well-trained young men in the United States why they do not apply to their churches for work in Africa. The reply almost always is that they've been told by their boards that the colonial governments do not want American Negroes as missionaries. From my own experience, I do not believe this is true. For a number of years the Belgian Congo government did in fact prohibit American Negroes from going to the colony, but I understand this prohibition has now been removed.

The present Episcopal Bishop of Liberia is an American Negro who has served in that high office since 1945.

The Seventh-Day Adventists courageously had a Negro missionary in South Africa for a while. He was B. W. Abney, and from all reports he did very well. While he was sent out specifically to work with the colored people of that country, he made friends with all segments of the population. That shows what a really humble Christian can do — "safe above life's raging sea."

I don't think I'm mistaken when I say that during all the years the Galangue station has been run by American and African Negroes there has never been a single occasion that one could point to with shame and say it was because of the race. I feel that the record of American Negroes in Galangue will always be a high-water mark in the missionary work in Angola. There has never been cause for anyone to charge that the Americans tried to influence the Africans to be anything more than good citizens. This is proved by the fact that they are always welcomed by the Portuguese authorities in Angola.

And today there are but few colonies where the all-Negro denominations are not serving. Moreover, in those in which they're not working, the reason is not their color but lack of funds.

The Foreign Mission Board, National Baptist, U.S.A. Inc., and other Negro Foreign Mission Boards are working in seven African colonies and countries. They have hundreds and thousands of students in their schools. Scores of students have been sent from Africa to America by their boards for higher education. Most of them have returned home to Africa as teachers, preachers, lawyers and doctors. Those who have chosen to remain in Europe or America have proved to be good and loyal citizens of their adopted lands.

Some interracial American churches have adopted a

policy of appointing missionaries without discrimination as
to race. They should certainly be commended for this,
but in areas like Africa and Asia where there is a special
place and need for missionaries of the African race this
policy is not farsighted enough. There needs to be a
wholehearted recognition of the superiority of the Negro
in this field and an all-out campaign to enlist his services.

It may seem remarkable that these Negro missionaries
can work so peacefully in Africa along with their European and American-trained staffs. Certainly no accusa-
tion of subversive teachings or acts has ever been brought
against them.

I have given deep thought to this subject and have come
to the conclusion that the secret must lie in the lessons that
the American Negro learned during the 250 years of
slavery. During that period of trial, I am convinced, the
Negro learned much of the essence of Christianity. He
learned how to work hard. He developed a sense of loyalty and humility and he learned to prize education and
thrift. Quite unintentionally, he picked up a lot of the
philosophy and psychology of the white man.

When the Negro goes to Africa he carries the lessons
he has learned back to his brethren in Africa. He has some
advantages over the white man in his dealings. For one
thing he does not have any social customs to guard against
because of race and background. Strangers and newcomers
always commented on the way the Africans moved in and
out of our house with ease, and always felt at home there
— a situation that does not always exist in white missions,
unfortunately. Natives can come in my front door and sit

anywhere they please. I felt I had an advantage in that my children could play with and grow up with the native youngsters. Many African children have been adopted by Negro missionaries and brought to this country and educated and sent back to Africa as missionaries. As a rule they make good workers.

The natives who have lived in the homes of American Negroes have learned the value of hard work and thrift. The initiative they display compared with that of other natives is noticeable.

There is a distinct advantage for the missionary who can walk into the native's home and sit down with him, eat parched corn from the same piece of broken pot, or roasted sweet potatoes out of the same fire. That is the time the African opens up his heart and drinks in the missionary's words as being true and not just part of a colonial trick to "pull the wool over his eyes."

Usually because of his limited financial means, the Negro missionary does not have too much to offer of this world's goods, but he does a lot of talking and wishing. The African, at least, knows that what the missionary has, he is willing and anxious to share.

When I discovered how eager the Africans were to learn the ways of the white man, it set me to thinking about what my people had learned during those 250 years of slavery. Certainly we had seen both the bad and the good side of the white man. Some of our people had risen high enough to become churchmen, scholars, teachers, presidents of colleges, doctors, farmers and businessmen. The Africans are conscious of the fact that there must be a pattern to such progress in such a short span of years.

I think it is this: At the very start, the American Negro learned to trust in God. He learned that God was as much his Saviour as the white man's.

Next he learned the value of honest toil. After he became a free man there was nothing for the American Negro to do but pull himself up by his bootstraps. He had no one to back him financially but he has come a long way through his own toil and sweat.

We are still learning the value of education and character building.

Arnold Toynbee, the British historian, has said that the white man in this twentieth century can learn something about religion from the Negro. Certainly if you look down the roster of outstanding American Negroes today you will find that most of them got their start and inspiration for an education at the feet of a Negro preacher or Sunday School teacher. Most of our leading Negro schools in America today are church-related institutions. I do not believe that anyone will question the American Negro's ability to build churches and religious leadership.

This deep religious faith may be an inheritance from the times of slavery. During those long hard years colored people turned to the Master because they needed Him, and they cannot forget that God is "an ever present help in time of trouble."

Then too, the black man knew and had a deep-seated faith that the Master would some way reward him for a clean heart and good deeds just as he would anyone else. So he plugged ahead not only to meet his own everyday needs but to attain a place for himself in the white man's economy. The Negro has been able to achieve these things in America because there were among the white men people who were good teachers and willing for the Negroes to have the best. Today many of those schools which were founded and run for many years by white missionaries have been turned over in many places to all Negro staffs. With the end of segregation now, they will open their doors to whites as well, furnishing a kind of "learning by doing" education that will be valuable to many white boys in lower income brackets.

One basic lesson the Negro has learned during his American education is that success comes in large measure through hard work. The Negro teacher is usually with his students not only in the classroom but in the home, fields and shops. It is well, too, not to overlook another factor that has made Negroes good teachers of their own people — the pride of race.

Hundreds of African students who have come to America under the auspices of Negro Foreign Mission Boards have carried back with them the same spirit of dedication to the job at hand.

Under the surface, the spiritual and cultural patterns of the African and American Negroes are the same. With proper funds, equipment and trained leaders they work together as brothers.

I think if the interracial churches of America would realize this their missionary work would take a big leap ahead not only in Africa but in many parts of the world. Today the missionary movement is at a crossroads. Even in places where they have done fine work, they are losing ground today because of the nationalist awakening among the people.

I am convinced after thirty years in Africa that the major part of the work in rural Africa should be carried on by American Negroes, working with the Africans. For one thing, they can work their way into the confidence of the older people who are the leaders in the rural villages. I have heard old men, talking among themselves, say: "A white man is a white man; it matters not where you find him." One of their proverbs says: "It never pays for a cockroach to try to make friends with a hen because sooner or later he is going to be eaten by the hen." The old men are always sitting around suspiciously weighing the words of the white missionaries. They weigh those of the Negro, too, but they soon come to the conclusion that we are one of them. Even when we cuss them out, they clap their hands and say we are doing it because we love them. That means they will drink in what the Negro missionary says. At present about ninety per cent of all of Africa's production is done by non-Christians and unlettered men and women. They need to be reached and treated not as poor benighted souls but as "God's children." The gap between pagan and Christian should not even be thought of in our efforts to develop these people. When a missionary makes this distinction he is retarding the evangelization of Africa and slamming the doors of the church in the faces of future great church leaders.

I do not mean to leave white men out of the picture. They should work side by side with the American Negroes, teaching in the schools and colleges of Africa, working in its hospitals and in its pulpits, but the Negroes should be the main interpreters of the white man to Africa.

China, India and Japan asked the Western Christian

Churches for Negro missionaries twenty-five or thirty years ago. They made it clear they were not asking for Negro missionaries because they had a better brand of religion but because they felt that Negro missionaries would understand them and their sufferings better, because they had gone through them and had come out a successful people.

The colored people of North America and the West Indies have been in direct contact with the white man for something over three hundred years now — in the fields, shops, schoolrooms, business and churches. During those years they have learned quite a bit about the arts of work, teaching, the sciences, the power of prayer and the way the white man's mind works. The Negro has sensed the qualities that have driven the white man ahead of other peoples.

The people of the East have not been blind to the progress of the colored people in the midst of enlightened white folk. It is not strange that they want the Negroes now to come over and help them.

Who can say that when those first twenty Negro slaves from Africa were landed at Jamestown, Virginia, in 1620 that it was not part of the plan of the Master that the offspring of those men should be the interpreters of the white man to the colored peoples of Africa and the East? The men who were the "Black Ivory" to American slaveholders may have had a higher destiny than has yet been generally realized.

I know from experience that nothing stirs the inner soul of a man more than hearing how an American Negro has "come up." It is best done at the dinnertable or while walking across the fields or while you are down in a ditch helping a brother. It is these intimate talks and words from a humble fellow man that really move men to action.

The African or Asian likes to hear about American Negroes whose fathers were butlers and whose mothers were washerwomen but who "came up" through high school and college. Indirectly these throw favorable light on the white man's way of life but at the same time they impress on the natives the value of hard work, study and prayers. Out of this approach I am convinced would grow strong churches and Christian nations and a better understanding between East and West.

The Negro should be used as a spearhead with which the white man's ideals and understanding would be driven deep into the heart of Africa and of Asia.

I am afraid that if the white man doesn't wake up soon to lost opportunities the African will have planted the idea throughout his continent that he has been sold down the river.

13

How Can I Sleep?

THIRTY YEARS' work as a missionary in Africa has convinced me that the Africans are fine people. Those in Angola among whom I worked know that lying and cheating are wrong. They are eager to learn and have shown outstanding ability in the classroom and workshop. They understand truth and they have knowledge of God. That the Christian mission finds it easy to build on.

What we need to do — and I say this to Africans, Europeans and Americans alike — is to roll up our sleeves and work together as a team. Mistakes have been made on both sides. Today some Africans want to see all white men driven from their lands. Some would use violence if necessary. They don't stop to realize that with the white man gone they would have neither the capital nor the knowhow to develop the rich resources of their countries.

On the other hand, the Word of God is going to make little progress in Africa so long as it is propagated only with foreign aid. It has to be planted with it, but should be propagated with real African sweat.

The white man must recognize that the future progress

of Africa will be forged out of a partnership built out of love for and appreciation of the African, and not founded upon a condescending idea that the African is some sort of inferior human being. The white man — American or European — must look upon the African as a man who has not had the opportunity of being trained. When both get onto this basis of understanding, then we will join hands and march forward together.

Today parts of Africa are in dire trouble. Take the situation in Johannesburg, for instance. I read of the walls and troubles that are being built up for the black man there with heavy heart. There are terrible portents there for social disturbance and disaster.

Yet as I look back over my thirty years' work among the Africans, I do not have the feeling that the problem is insoluble. Thomas Carlyle once said: "All labor, whether it be of the hand or the head, is divine." That must be the key to the solution of Africa's problem.

I wrote to President Buell Gallagher of Talladega College in 1939: "When the Africans are trained to work, and above all learn how to develop and get the most out of the soil, then and then only the Africans and Africa are going to be developed."

Today young men from the neighborhood of our mission in Portuguese West Africa go on foot to Johannesburg, fifteen hundred miles away. They go there to work in order to earn money to buy a portable sewing machine, a Victrola or bicycle. Yet if they had been taught the simple science of farming, an occupation they are cut out for, right at home, they could have earned the money right there to spend in any of the cities of Angola.

The pull of economic opportunity in the big cities is terrific these days. To try to meet it in Johannesburg or any other of those end points instead of back on the farm is like trying to dam up the Mississippi River somewhere in the neighborhood of New Orleans. One might be able to build a dam large enough to check the onrush of waters for a while but in time the river would burst right through it.

To put in a permanent dam that will effectively control the water we must go way back up the tributaries and change their courses. Then the building of a dam at the mouth of the river will be easy.

That should be the aim of any government program or self-help measures that are tried out in Africa in the next ten or fifteen years.

As you can see on a map of Angola there are thousands of good roads throughout the country, but still transportation for the average farmer who wants to get his corn, beans and wheat to the market is limited. Trucks can go out from the city only so far and make a profit on a load. That distance is around two hundred miles. Outside of that radius today there is practically no farming. Rich land is going to waste and people are hungry unnecessarily. The answer is perfectly obvious, and like many easy solutions to big problems it seems to be ignored by many economic experts, who are apt to think in terms of large-scale mechanization: all that is needed is enough oxcarts to carry the produce to the end of the truck routes. At Galangue we have made a start in manufacturing these carts but there is room for many missions like ours, if they would undertake such work.

If we as missionaries and others who really want to help the Africans would go all out in teaching them how to develop the things they already have in their hands and around them, we could, I am convinced, eliminate the dangerous congestion in the big cities, especially in South Africa, and stop any threat of communism right in its tracks.

You can't tell me there is any reason at all why people who are by nature pastoral and agricultural should starve in Africa or have to go without employment adequate to meet their everyday needs for food and clothing. I know of one man in Africa today who has as high as ten thousand head of cattle — but all of his farm work is being done with just one small hoe. Because of all those cattle he is considered a wealthy man by all his fellow tribesmen, yet he lives on the brink of starvation. His shoulders furnish the only means of transportation he has for getting his crops to market, and if nothing is done he, like countless other Africans, will trudge through an entire lifetime sick, footsore and hungry, weighted under the cruel burden of hundred-pound bags of wheat. When more of these peo ple can be taught to build oxcarts and to forge simple plows these conditions will be eliminated and we will have the beginnings of many flourishing communities. Overnight we will see growing up from the good, healthy roots of Africa thousands of self-supporting schools and churches and well-paid teachers and preachers who can show those people the path to more happy and prosperous lives.

The Africans can't do the job without outside help, both in ideas and money. I have lots of dreams for my friends in Africa. Sometimes perhaps I get too enthusiastic but

I think generally I understand what they need and just how much of a dose they can take at one time. I have learned some pretty hard lessons in Africa myself, since the time I went there as an eager young missionary bent on showering them with the Word of God. I was soon told to back up and help these people get rid of the pain of hunger in their stomachs. Then they were more willing to accept God's promises.

First thing that needs to be done for the Africans is to teach them the simple skills of wheelwrighting and blacksmithing. A hundred ordinary forges in my Galangue area with three young men training at each would work a remarkable transformation in the area's economy. Courses in blacksmithing must be carried out at control points in line with the daily needs of the people. They need to be trained in the making and ironing-off of wheelbarrow, oxcarts, plows, hoes, axes and all kinds of hand tools. As the demand grows in the villages for farm equipment there will be all kinds of hand tools which they do not have today.

If you enter the home of an African native today, you will find something that can be called a chair, but there is generally no table or bed. It is not unusual these days to see a $75 imported bicycle standing in the living room but many items that even the lowest paid worker in Europe and America considers a necessity just are not there. It is apparent that carpentry is one of the trades that most needs to be taught in missionary schools. Village night school courses in this art would also be most welcome.

There needs to be a system of agricultural extension work set up that would call in village men twice a year to give training in the use of the ox and the plow, how to make a compost pile, how to use green manure, how to drain the river bottoms and how to care for livestock.

For those who are too far away to attend school there should be extension workers in the village equipped with teams of oxen, oxcarts, plows, yokes, bow chains and shovels who will be teaching the people. The ox must be a factor in the development of rural Angola. Every village should have its teams to teach others how to plow with oxen. It takes about four weeks, I figure, to train a pair of oxen, and two weeks to teach a young man to handle the ox and to plow.

I should think an extension worker could stay in a given area about two months and then go on to another area about fifty miles farther into the interior. The Africans are just beginning to wear shoes. Therefore, there is a big opportunity and need for courses in both tanning and shoemaking. In Angola wonderful hides are available, not only from the many cattle but from the animal known as an eland which is a kind of antelope. These animals grow to a height of about six feet and sometimes weigh as much as two thousand pounds, so you can imagine how much hide there is on just one. Then we have trees that produce as high as twenty per cent in tannic acid.

Today hundreds of tons of hides are destroyed by insects and worms in the villages of the interior; if they could be tanned it would mean a great saving to the people and would provide a new source of income. Shoe leather sells at approximately 60 cents a pound in Angola. There is no reason why, with some guidance and a starter subsidy perhaps, the larger cattle raisers of Angola should not play a part in the new birth of the African village. If we had the tanning vats, it would not be long before we would be turning out 300 to 400 tons of leather per year. Then we would be able not only to fill the growing local demand for shoes but we could develop a market in Portugal and other European countries. If we were able to get hold of the proper craftsmen, we could also go in for leather art work and handbags. With these we would find a ready market since African art is a much appreciated novelty today in leading cities around the world.

With the introduction of ceramics and pottery in our area, we would not only have the basis for a lucrative industry but a means of developing another type of native African art. Many native art forms are already passing out of existence. They must be brought back through encouragement and inducement before it is too late. It doesn't take much imagination to foresee the day when Angola will have a flourishing ceramics industry that will benefit the whole continent of Africa.

Since cotton and flax grow well in Angola, especially in the southern part and in the basins of the Cunene and Cubangu Rivers, there is a great need for teaching the people how to weave. At present some of them wear clothes made of bark and think these are more stylish than those of cloth, but all textiles used by the people of Angola today are imported. A home industry in this field would mean a big saving in money for the natives. At present the only sheep there are in Angola are wool-less, but they could be crossbred with wool-bearing sheep and in two generations they would be producing good wool. Mr. K. H. Prior and the Portuguese government have made some experiments along this line with encouraging results.

Foundry work is another field in which there are tremendous crying needs in Africa. The people need to learn modern ways of making such simple equipment as pots, skillets, Dutch ovens, hand-powered gristmills, corn shellers, wagon skeins and bushings, plows, church bells, small cooking stoves and other everyday items that people in Europe and America have long taken for granted. These simple items would work a revolution in the average family's life in Angola.

Most startling of all opportunities for advancement in Africa is in the field of farming. Why, in Angola today there are places where the top soil is ten feet or more deep. Yet it has never seen or heard a plow. Just think what one could do in that country with about a dozen tractors!

Sometimes I sit and dream about the changes that could be wrought. Of course, it will take considerable sweat. Bringing about a basic change in any people is a backbreaking job and one that takes patience and more patience. At least that has been my experience in Africa. But the satisfaction you get out of the result is worth every drop that falls from your brow in the process. I can tell you that — from my heart.

Suppose I tell myself I could plant 500 acres of land in corn, beans, wheat, peanuts and soy beans. These as well as rice, oats, barley, buckwheat and millet, grow well in all parts of the colony. Corn, wheat and rice are exported to Europe. The other cereals could be grown to an exporting volume, if the natives were given seeds and a market for them was found.

That valley land in Angola will produce not less than fifty to seventy-five bushels of corn per acre, and other crops in the same abundant proportions. With 500 acres under cultivation, our mission's net income the first year would be something like $35,000. Then perhaps, with some more sweat and toil, we could increase our acreage until it reaches 1000 acres of general farm crops.

Then would be the time to put in 100 acres each of vegetables, fruits, sisal, coffee and similar "luxury" crops. Cotton and flax do well in the eastern and southern part of the colony. The government has distributed flaxseed to Portuguese settlers and to missionaries in various parts of the colony and they did well. As yet the natives have not been taught to grow these crops. Cotton is grown by Europeans on the plantation system. I could go on.

There is no doubt about it, Angola is a paradise for the Point IV man or the missionary who wants to work in the soil and teach the African natives to do the same. If a man has other ideas, such as of walking in and trying to rob the country of its natural resources, or give the native something he does not want, I would advise him to stay at home.

With help, Africa could go in heavily for dairying. Point IV men need to give courses in the care of milk, butter and cheese making. There would be an unlimited market for their products. In order to teach the natives how to use milk and butter to advantage, I would like to see a system of dairy sheds set up in all parts of Angola. At each of these there would be stationed men who know how to process the milk, take proper care of the cattle and are familiar with the dairy business generally. In each area there would be built two dipping tanks for livestock and two silos at each dairy barn. Also at each shed there should be at least three registered bulls for breeding. Tractors and ox teams would be maintained there for plowing and other work. In the southern part of the colony today both horses and mules are found, but they are not being used by the natives as work animals as yet.

The cattle would be pastured by their individual owners but brought to the community sheds for milking. Some help would need to be given the people in developing good grazing land by showing them how to plant alfalfa and other good pasture crops. I am sure the Africans will welcome this experiment in co-operative dairying with open arms because they are great lovers of anything having to do with cattle. When the people of Africa begin to milk their cows and are able to process the milk, we shall see better fed children and less sickness among them. Money now being spent for medicine can be put into something else.

Oil-bearing plants thrive in Angola, but today you will not find 100 pounds of fats of any kind in a single village. There is a big opportunity in the co-operative planting of such oil-bearing plants as peanuts and soy beans. Presses would be needed to extract the oil in various localities. With a little organization, a surplus of oil would probably be available that could be shipped to the fish canneries or used for overseas export. In Angola we even use castor oil in our automobiles. The proportion used is one part castor oil to three parts regular motor oil.

Today canning of fruits and vegetables is unknown among the Africans. Their soil is capable of growing the year round something that could be canned. Grapefruit, peaches, apples, berries and pineapples grow well in the colony. Since the people all live in villages it would not be difficult to develop canning factories among them. They only need someone to distribute the seeds for the produce to be canned and give directions on how to cultivate them. The Africans will follow such instructions to the letter and will bring the vegetables to the cannery. They will walk in from five to ten miles around, I know.

The coastal plains of Africa would be ideal for fruit growing, but the rainfall is light and there would have to be irrigation as there is in Southern California.

Something needs to be done about better houses. Limestones, good clays, timber and building stones can be found in all parts of the colony. Since the African natives are used to living in villages, a building plan on a co-operative basis should not be difficult to develop. I have a plan in the back of my head now for the setting aside of tracts of about 1000 acres or more. These I would divide up into farms of 15 to 25 acres. Each plot would be given to a family with the understanding that they would cultivate it. We would break it up for them with a tractor but they, when their crops were in, would have to pay us for the gasoline used in the tractor. Each year the family would set aside a certain amount of money toward a home building fund. As soon as the fund equals half the cost of the new house we would come in with our trade classes and start to build. In these classes simple building construction would be taught, including the making and laying of bricks. When the community is all built, we from the mission would come in and erect a schoolhouse and make it a branch of our mission school.

In our part of Africa, the termites are very bad. Almost anything valuable you have you must store in iron boxes so it won't be eaten up. This means all of our buildings must be of brick and we will need tile roofs and floors to keep out other pests. As I plan it, each house would have three to four rooms and a detached kitchen. All homes will have running water which will aid in the fight against dysentery. If possible we will put lights in them too. In order to keep the cost as low as possible, we will get the men of the community to do the common labor such as digging the foundations and hauling the rocks and building materials.

Dozens of young men need to be trained for the work of village sanitation and equipped with tools to help them drain the swamps and fill in the holes and low places in the villages and around the houses. The traditional "stick and dirt" houses need to be replastered every three years so they will not become dens for bugs. Special effort needs to be exercised to insure good sources for drinking water. As it is now, any place in the stream will do for the African. Often this is below the village where all the filth of the land and people has found its way. At the outset of the rainy season there are outbreaks of dysentery which cause the death of many children and old folks every year. Places should be established above the village for the taking of drinking water and enclosed so the hogs cannot get into them. The people need to be shown how to dig wells and taught where to put them.

Dr. William S. Gilchrist, of the Canadian-American Board mission at Dondi, has been very successful in the bore-hole type of toilets in Angola but there are not enough of these yet. Septic tanks could be used, too.

This may seem like a big undertaking but with just a little money I could build a few sample houses — say ten miles apart around Galangue. They would attract a lot of attention and work wonders in creating a desire for better homes among the natives.

Then I would work out carefully the price of each house, translating it into terms of so many pigs, or cattle, or bushels of corn or beans. Then the natives could visualize just how much work they would need to do in order to get one of those houses. In a couple of years, by the time say two crops had matured, we would have plenty of buyers, I am sure.

Since the mainstay of the native diet is still corn meal mush, there is much that needs to be taught the native women about simple nutrition. I think this could best be started in a community kitchen where the women of each village could come for training in cooking, plain sewing and other household arts. I would like to see a "super kitchen" erected — 200 to 300 feet long and 25 feet wide. On each side I would place small simple kitchen units, 10 by 10 feet.

In Africa none of us aspire to such luxuries as electric refrigerators or deep freezes, or even gas stoves for that matter. Each unit in the model kitchen would have a fireplace for cooking, a table, a couple of chairs and a sideboard for dishes. Three women would work in each unit and they would live together at the school for the duration of the course — six weeks. Aside from cooking and general housekeeping, plain sewing and washing and ironing would also be taught. Later on, I would hope that the villages round about would all build their own community kitchens and the families of the women would come there to eat while they were going to school. Produce for the training courses would come out of the school garden.

In the short space of three or four years we would have quite an army of Angola women with a wide knowledge of housekeeping. While the lessons they would be taught seem elementary to people from more advanced countries, they would open a whole new world to these women, ready today for a great new awakening.

Not long ago I was returning home late one night from a preaching mission. At midnight I passed through the village of Gongo, four miles from our mission. As we walked through that quiet town my companion suddenly called my attention to a strange thing — not a baby in Gongo was crying.

"Why should the babies be crying?" I asked with some surprise. "Coles," he replied, "they are not crying because their mothers and fathers have learned to work as you have been teaching them." Sure enough, later on I had occasion to pass through a village where the people had not learned to work the river bottom with the plows and hoes we brought them. There the babies were hungry and crying constantly. Some of them were not even able to cry. They only whimpered.

For the youngsters of Angola, a brighter future is already in store. It isn't a dream. Soon I shall be laying the foundation for the Pestalozzi Children's Shelter (Agricultural and Industrial School for Orphans and Destitute Children) of Angola, Portuguese West Africa.

Our plan is to gather in orphans and destitute children from all parts of Angola. Normally I think it is better to have the children remain in their villages with their own people or tribe until they have gotten their Bible training in their own language and their grammar school work. But our youngsters will be those who are without any family at all. Somewhere we shall have to acquire bedding, eating utensils, milk bottles, tools for handicrafts and so forth.

As soon as those kids are old enough we will expect them to help milk the cows, look after the chickens, pigs and ducks, and work in the garden just as I did in my boyhood days in Alabama. We will keep them until they are eighteen and by then will expect them to be able to make their own way by both their hand and their brain.

Another group that my heart goes out to especially are the women of Angola. They sit there on boulders and flat rocks in the bush — pounding, always pounding, the grain to make meal for their menfolk. Carefully they tend and turn the grain until it gets dry, but often a stiff wind comes and blows a good portion of it away. When the weather is bad, they pound indoors with a heavy mortar and pestle.

About half their day is taken up preparing meal that could be ground in a few minutes with a hand-powered gristmill. And such a mill would be so easy to come by.

In Africa the women still do most of the work in the fields. I shall never forget with what joy a group of them greeted my first demonstration of a plow on those rich river-bottom lands. They clapped their hands and jumped up and down shouting, "Look — the ox is drawing the hoe."

When I started talking to the Africans about the plow back in 1923 the missionaries scoffed at me. "Sam," they said, "the little black woman with the little hoe can beat you farming."

I turned on them and said: "When I see that little black gal well fed, with clothes enough on to hide her nakedness, then I will believe that."

One of our mission men recently saw a strange sight in a field near the mission. A man and his wife were plowing. The man was carrying the baby on his back while the wife was leading the oxen. This, we presumed, was because the oxen might endanger the baby. In the old days the woman would have been hoeing with the baby on her back. At least this is a change in old patterns and a step toward less bondage for Africa's womanhood, and a better chance of survival for her child.

Then there are the old folks. Even though they work hard at the backbreaking job of plowing and hoeing, who is going to take their wheat to the market?

One night not long ago, Deacon Simon of the village of Ndala came to see me. I asked him about his wheat. Bent and gray, he looked at me. "Mr. Coles," he said slowly, "I have ten bags of wheat, each weighing two hundred pounds. That is a whole ton of wheat — a fortune if I can get it to market." He went on: "But look at me. My wife and I are now old. Our children are gone. How can we possibly take ten bags of wheat to the market on our shoulders?"

What could I tell this old man? Indeed, there was no answer — yet. Some day there must be.

"That, Deacon Simon," I said quietly, "is my problem."

That night when I went to bed I couldn't sleep. As I lay there some lines of poetry formed themselves in my thought. I guess that great leader, General Armstrong, who urged more work and less song and poetry for the Negro, will forgive me if I record them here:

> *How can I sleep?*
> *When the poor African women*
> *Are toiling over the rugged mountains*
> *Bruising their feet*
> *Carrying their wheat*
> *To the distant markets —*
> *How can I sleep?*
>
> *How can I sleep?* .
> *When you can track the carriers*
> *By stains from their bleeding feet*
> *Carrying their burden to the distant markets*
> *To the distant markets —*
> *How can I sleep?*

What can we do to help them?
To save their weary feet?
They who carry the wheat
Over the distant mountains?

Oxcarts for their burdens
Oxcarts for the wheat
Oxcarts for the journey
Will save their bruised feet.

Yes, they shall have oxcarts
Carts and oxen both.
With hammer, forge and anvil
We'll build those carts and wheels
To carry their burdens heavy
Over the distant mountains —

Oh, the pain of these bleeding feet
How can I sleep?